RISE

OF THE
UNDERDOG

DANNY HIGGINBOTHAM

RISE
OF THE
UNDERDOG

Sport Media ◉

underdog

noun un.der.dog

: a person, team, etc., that is expected to
lose a contest or battle

: a less powerful person or thing
that struggles against a more powerful
person or thing

*'Our greatest glory is not in never falling,
but in rising every time we fall'*

This story is dedicated to my family and the people
who have helped me along the way.

You know who you are.

Sport Media

**Danny Higginbotham:
Rise Of The Underdog**

© Danny Higginbotham

Written with Wayne Barton.

First Edition
Published in Great Britain in 2015.

Published and produced by: Trinity Mirror Sport Media,
PO Box 48, Old Hall Street, Liverpool L69 3EB.

Managing Director: Steve Hanrahan
Commercial Director: Will Beedles
Executive Editor: Paul Dove
Executive Art Editor: Rick Cooke
Senior Marketing Executive: Claire Brown
Sales and Marketing Manager: Elizabeth Morgan

ISBN: 9781908695994

Photographic acknowledgements:
Front cover image: Tony Woolliscroft
Other images: Phil Greig, PA Photos,
Danny Higginbotham collection.

Printed and bound by CPI Group (UK) Ltd,
Croydon, CR0 4YY.

Contents

Acknowledgements   9

Career statistics   11

Foreword: Tony Pulis   13

1.   Running On Empty   17
2.   Blackstrap Molasses   27
3.   You're Finished   37
4.   School Of United   47
5.   Banned   63
6.   Copacabana   79
7.   Ram Raid   95
8.   Down And Out   109
9.   The Imposter   127
10.   Blurred Lines   139

11. Saints & Sinners   149

12. Battersea Dogs Home   163

13. Back With Roy   177

14. Great Expectations   189

15. Going Home   199

16. Stoke v Arsenal   213

17. As Good As It Gets   227

18. Dear Diary   237

19. End Of An Era   251

20. The Rock   265

21. Winners & Losers   275

Career profile   287

Acknowledgements

I'm very thankful to everyone I've worked with throughout my career. First of all, I'm so grateful for the upbringing Manchester United gave me in the sport and I'd like to think that I've carried the values I learned and was taught at Old Trafford with me throughout my career.

It almost goes without saying that, of course, I also thank Derby County, Southampton, Stoke City, Sunderland, Nottingham Forest, Ipswich Town, Sheffield United, Chester City, Altrincham and all the people involved at Gibraltar for their support and contribution to my development and achievements as a professional.

To be able to play in North East, East Midlands and South Coast derby games has been a privilege, as has the opportunity to play in as many competitions as I have – the Champions League, Europa League, the FA Cup, the World Club Championship, the League Cup, FA Cup, Championship, Premier League, even playing in the Conference and being involved in finals that I sadly wasn't lucky enough to play in. I punched above my weight for a long time, but that was down to my desire and commitment.

I have to give the deepest gratitude to Sir Alex Ferguson, who not only taught me how to behave and act a footballer but so much about being a man, too. Tony Pulis taught me so much, more than any other, about how to improve my game as a defender… the biggest compliment I can give Tony is that when I hear myself speaking now, I hear so much of him and the way he spoke. I learned so much from him and I also want to thank him for doing me the honour of writing the foreword for this book. I do, also, want to place on record my thanks to every manager I played for, as all of them gave me valuable experience in the game.

The most important people to thank are my family – my parents who sacrificed so much, my wife and my children. I consider myself very fortunate that all four of my children were able to see me play football.

Thanks also to my true friends – John McKeown, Kaz (aka Skip), Charles Heathcoate, Lee Thompson, Rory Delap and Andy Griffin, to name just a few who I've met throughout my career. Apart from my three team-mates I've just mentioned, I've been very fortunate to have the above mentioned people away from football to help keep me grounded.

Finally, I would like to thank Alex Black, a fantastic agent and friend who has always looked after my best interests; Wayne Barton, who helped me write this book; Andy Hipkiss and James Hancock for all of his support as well as all at Trinity Mirror for their help.

Danny Higginbotham, 2015

Career stats

Manchester United
1 Aug 1995-5 July 2000
Appearances: 7, Goals: 0

Derby County
5 July 2000-31 Jan 2003
Appearances: 98, Goals: 4

Southampton
31 Jan 2003-3 Aug 2006
Appearances: 106, Goals: 4

Stoke City
3 Aug 2006-29 Aug 2007
Appearances: 48, Goals: 7

Sunderland
29 Aug 2007-2 Sept 2008
Appearances: 22, Goals: 3

Stoke City
2 Sept 2008-1 Jan 2013
Appearances: 80, Goals: 7

Sheffield United
1 Jan 2013-31 Aug 2013
Appearances: 18, Goals: 0

(Loan)

Royal Antwerp: 1 Nov 1998-30 Jun 1999 – Appearances: 32, Goals: 4
Nottingham Forest: 31 Jan 2012-19 Apr 2012 – Appearances: 6, Goals: 1.
Ipswich Town: 1 Sept 2012-31 Dec 2012 – Appearances: 12 ,Goals: 0

(Non-League)
Chester City (2013-2014): Appearances: 17, Goals: 1
Altrincham (2013-2014): Appearances: 2, Goals: 0.
Gibraltar (2013-2014): Appearances: 3, Goals: 0.

Career total (including non-league & loan)
Appearances: 451, Goals: 31

About the co-author

Wayne Barton, who helped Danny write this book, has ghost-written numerous autobiographies of renowned sportsmen, actors and musicians.

A lifelong Manchester United supporter, like Danny, Wayne has worked with famous Old Trafford names including Brian Greenhoff, Gordon Hill, Tommy Docherty, Martin Buchan, Sammy McIlroy, Harry Gregg and Mick Duxbury. He is the football columnist for international broadcaster Setanta Sports and has been described by the Independent as 'the leading writer on Manchester United on the period between Sir Matt Busby and Sir Alex Ferguson'.

Additionally, Wayne has worked in Hollywood and across the USA with names including Charles Baker, from the monster hit TV show 'Breaking Bad'.

Foreword by Tony Pulis

Danny first came to my attention as a player when he was a young lad; I'd recognised his potential and always felt that he would go on to be someone who would show great consistency. That, of course, proved to be the case.

It didn't take long, after the first time I signed him for Stoke City in 2006, for Danny to establish himself in terms of importance. He quickly became a building block for everything that the club has since achieved; I feel it's imperative to mention just how important his contribution was to the success of the club while I was there.

As a manager, when you go into a football club you try and put players in place early on who will be the foundations, integral to the long-term plan of what you're hoping to achieve, and Danny was certainly one of those.

He had many qualities which I admired. First and foremost, and most importantly, I felt he was a very good player, and was very underrated. He conducted himself fantastically; he had a great way about him and instantly became a great person to have in the dressing room.

A hardworking, diligent, good professional, I knew that if ever a time came when things weren't going so well, Danny would be one of the first I would be able to call upon to step up and be counted. Fair, honest and uncompromising – characteristics of Danny Higginbotham which became the hallmark of Stoke City Football Club.

He was a leader in the dressing room and also a fantastic example to younger players; the way he carried himself set the standard as a senior player to the younger ones like Ryan Shawcross to learn from. Danny captained the team and led by example – it's very important for managers to have players to rely on and he was certainly one of those.

We never really wanted to lose Danny when Sunderland came in, but the money they offered was difficult for us to turn down, as was the opportunity for Danny at the time.

When the chance came to re-sign him when we were promoted in 2008, I didn't have to think twice. I was delighted to get him back and in his second spell at the Britannia he went from strength to strength, cementing his position in Stoke City folklore.

The term 'legend' is overused, in my opinion, but all things in football are relative and it's very easy to see why Stoke supporters would describe Danny as a legend for the club for everything he accomplished in his 128 appearances there. The group of players we had in that period will always be revered and looked upon with great affection and Danny was a key part of that group.

It was, of course, tremendously disappointing for him to miss the FA Cup final of 2011 after he had scored that great goal to ensure we qualified for the semi-final. I was desperately sad for him, but his time at Stoke City – and, indeed, his career – will be defined by the wholehearted way he approached every game and the determination he showed rather than the sad events of April 2011. There are many things I admire about Danny, but one of the best things, as a manager, was that I could always trust him.

He was a great person to be around and to have around – he was a first-class professional and lad.

Clubs, and players, sometimes have a period in history where they are forever connected for what they achieved together – and it is fitting that Danny is seen as one of the most important players for Stoke City in the period in which he played because he was, quite simply, a manager's dream.

Tony Pulis, 2015

01

Running On Empty

Gainsborough. 9.45pm. Tuesday, January 7th, 2014. That's when I made the decision. The Altrincham team in which I was playing had just been defeated 5-4 but it wasn't the result, the team, the league or the state of the Gainsborough ground which had made my mind up – that was just the straw that broke the camel's back.

I used to get such a buzz in the build-up. On the day of a game, regardless of the level I was playing at or who we were playing against, I used to be so pumped up. It wasn't a choice, it was just the way it was. I didn't want to speak to anyone, my whole body would be crazy. I'd go to the toilet five or six times such was my adrenaline; then the game would start, be over, and I could be a completely different person again.

Now, I no longer had that desire.

If I'm being honest, I'd been feeling disillusioned for a long time. It wasn't the same. I'd been searching for something for quite a while that just wasn't there anymore and, on reflection, it was a decision that I should probably have taken quite a while earlier.

When I left Sheffield United at the start of the 2013/2014 season, I had a year left on my contract and that should have told me; I had no interest in the full time game anymore, the regimented procedures, the hotels, the nights before games. I'd just had enough.

I've always said that I know what my strengths and weaknesses are and the minute I was not fully committed on the pitch; the minute I was fearful of going into a tackle because of getting hurt; the minute I wouldn't run through a brick wall... that would be the time my career was finished.

I've not been the most gifted technically, I've always been honest enough to admit that. What gave me a decent career was that I'd put my body on the line. The natural thing for people to say when they're coming to the end is that their legs have gone, but for me, my head went. When that goes, your legs may as well have gone anyway; running ten or 20 yards may as well have been 30 or 40 because it just wasn't something I wanted to do anymore.

It wasn't that I wanted to feel this way, it was just the way it was... I'm sure that other footballers who finish on their terms are the ones who can deal with it a lot better than those who get their careers cut short because they can't find a club or they've had an injury.

Getting to 35 was a big thing for me. It was nothing to do with qualifying for my players' pension, I just always saw it as an achievement to get to that age and still be playing football – and then when I finally got there, I was like, "Well I'm here now. What next?" I wasn't enjoying it anymore.

I went from full-time to part-time to try and get my love of the game back. I thought with maybe not training as much, I might miss it and look forward to playing more than I had been. And that worked for a month or two but I got an injury in December which meant I spent Christmas with my family. It was a nice feeling to do that for the first time in about 15 years.

To celebrate Christmas Day with my children was fantastic; a far cry from 'come on kids, open your presents and then Dad's got to go to training' or 'let's have a bit of dinner and then I'll rush off to the hotel'. When you're playing, for the benefit you get, it's a small price to pay, but this Christmas I loved it and football wasn't on my mind. I wasn't gutted I wasn't playing Boxing Day. Not gutted that I wouldn't be back for the game on the 28th.

And that was unlike me – when I'd been injured before, I'd been desperate to get back.

As soon as the Gainsborough game ended I was on the phone to my wife and then my mum and dad to tell them that was it. Dad was great and said that if I'd told them a year ago I was finishing they'd have been so proud of me – he said it was my choice and there was nothing I could do if the time had come but he advised me to sleep on it and let the dust settle. My wife had heard it from me before – over the last year I'd mentioned it two or three times.

On the Wednesday morning after the game, I got advice from different people. I texted Michael Duberry and asked him:

"How do you know when the time's right?" He said "When your effort is more than the satisfaction you're getting back." I was still trying but I can concede that it might not have looked that way because my heart just wasn't in it.

There was no reward, no satisfaction, and Michael's advice resonated with me. I spoke to Richard Cresswell and Rory Delap, both good friends who had also recently retired, and their advice was similar. "Danny – you sound like you're at that point where you've had enough."

I've been friends with Rory for about 15 years and I think we're similar minded people; he said that throughout our careers we'd always put other people first, we'd played through injuries when we shouldn't have, and now was the time to put my family and myself first. He's one of the most selfless people I've ever met so for him to say that hit home.

I called my football agent, though, to be honest, his role on that side had dwindled. I'd negotiated the last two moves by myself as they were straightforward. He said that he knew this time was coming from the minute I left Sheffield United.

I wasn't enjoying it at Bramall Lane as I felt David Weir's ideas weren't really geared to senior professionals. I didn't fall out with anyone but didn't really get the opportunity. I respected him as much as anyone I worked under as he was my manager but I think he found it difficult asking for help from the senior players – that's just my opinion. I wasn't playing and the four hour round trip to just train with the kids wasn't for me.

Then, when I was at Chester Zoo with the family, I got a call asking me if I'd like to go to Notts County for a few months. They tried to entice me by saying they'd be playing Liverpool in the cup. Again, no disrespect intended, but I said 'no' without thinking about it. Notts County are a big club but I'd had enough of full-time football.

I heard of interest at Chester so I went to watch a game. I took my eldest lad and as we left and got in the car, I asked him what he thought of me going there to play, and he said it'd be great as he could come and watch me.

My first game was at Wrexham away; they hadn't beaten them for a few years and we won 2-0. Chester took around 900 fans – one of them parked next to me at the ground and said before the match, "Danny, you have the chance to make yourself a legend at this club after just one game."

When I got back to my car there was a piece of paper under the windshield wiper saying, 'See Danny, told you you'd become a legend'. I got immense satisfaction from that, I have to admit. It was a great feeling, but then after a month or so, I started losing that passion once again.

I moved to Altrincham from Chester in the hope that it would give me a bit of a pick-up. Altrincham was more than football to me; I'd grown up there, and I'd promised plenty of people I'd finish my career there. But as we finished our first game, a home game against Leamington where we won 3-2 with a late goal, I thought to myself, "What are you doing, Danny? It's gone."

I felt nothing, but I should.

I want to make it clear that it was nothing to do with the level I was playing at. I enjoyed my time right at the top and I'd enjoyed it lower down the leagues; to me, it was simply a game of football, it didn't matter if there was 40,000 or 400 fans there.

After my mind was made up, the next step was to announce

the decision but not before talking to my manager at Altrincham, Lee Sinnott. I thought he would try to convince me to stay on and see the season out.

I said I'd had enough and he just asked me to talk him through my last year. I told him how things had become monotonous, training was a chore, and Lee's response was simply, "You're done aren't you?"

I spoke to a man called John who worked for the club but also wrote for the Daily Mail, as he was going to handle the release. He sent me a copy of it before it went to print and it really touched me, the way it was done. The reaction I got was overwhelming – 99.9 per cent of it was people respecting and appreciating the decision.

It was important to me that people understood and that they knew I wasn't trying to bullshit anyone. I didn't want to take the piss out of the club or the fans, I didn't want to go through the motions and leave people with a different idea of me.

That evening was a very emotional one – my wife asked me why, if I felt I'd made a mistake, but my explanation of it was just that it was the end of an era. Other than my brother, my mum and my dad, football had been my longest friend.

The entire landscape of football has changed completely from when I first took my steps into it. The abolition of apprenticeships was the biggest key to change and it was too much, too quickly. I'm not on about your Wayne Rooneys, Sterlings, Ramseys, Wilsheres – your 18-year-olds who have come into the first team and made a real impact. Good luck to them – they deserve what they get for proving themselves.

Where it's gone wrong is with the 17 and 18-year-olds who

are nowhere near first teams and they're getting ridiculous amounts of money. They get a big contract because they're progressing well but they haven't made the first team yet; a four year contract takes them up to 22, and I'm not saying they all do it, but many take their foot off the gas. It's the best contract they're ever going to have. At 22, when they've stagnated, and drop down the leagues, they take a massive pay cut and get a reality check. It's a massive problem in the game.

It wound me up when I was in full-time football, although never caused such disillusion that it would influence my decision whether to carry on or not. It just confirmed that times were changing and it was a different game from the one I'd entered.

At Chester, we had a number of young lads who came to the club. John Rooney, younger brother of Wayne, was one of those, and what a character – it must just be a 'Rooney' trait. I've got all the time in the world for him – training was like a game, and it didn't bother me that he could be aggressive in the challenge in practice because I know if I'd have done it back he'd have been fine with it. He's one from a good mould but there's the other extreme of a young lad we had whose name I can't remember (which probably says it all). In his first game, he 'cashed' one of the opposition players off.

As an older player I've always tried to give advice and help to the youngsters. But I thought, 'Fuck you, you're done'. What was he doing? I couldn't speak to him after that.

I've played with players who have earned millions and millions and I've been fortunate enough to have done well from the game myself but I would never in my wildest dreams ever say anything like that to anyone. Here's an 18-year-old kid, on loan from a Championship club, doing it to players working their balls off in non-league. I had situations in games at non-league level where people would try and wind me up but I'd end up just laughing along with them and at the end of the game they'd be saying it was good to meet me. People try things but I don't have time for it; whether it's an opponent or a team-mate.

When I was at Sheffield United there was a time we were getting changed and I was approached by a young lad who was okay, he had a decent work ethic and everything. He'd seen my watch and liked it so asked how much it cost me. "How much do you think?" I asked. "Eight or nine grand?" then "fifteen grand" and then "twenty grand" he asked as I said 'no'. When I told him it cost £250 I asked him what did it matter?

There was a similar situation at Ipswich, when I arrived at the training ground in my big family wagon. I've never been that into cars, but each to their own, footballers are in a position that if they like fancy cars and watches, good luck to them.

As I'm walking into training one of the guys is looking down at me from the roof and says "Danny, all these lads come in Mercedes and BMWs and Range Rovers. Why the fuck are you driving a Volkswagen? You've had a decent career, what are you driving that for?" Maybe it's the perception of footballers these days but it's a materialistic thing that never makes sense to me. You have a nice car because you want to, not because somebody expects you to.

I've not been one for doing something just because that's what's expected; and I suppose when you look at the last 12 months of my playing career that much is plain to see. If I'm to put it bluntly, I tried my best and failed to recapture the buzz of playing football. I'd been told a long time ago that you're a long time retired and, with that in mind, I wanted to exhaust every avenue. I needed to make sure that when I decided to retire, I'd tried my absolute best to get that feeling back and when I finally did, I was able to look myself in the mirror and know that I had.

Once I made the decision, I can honestly say I haven't missed playing for one minute. The Saturday after I retired, I was able to go and watch my son play football for the first time in what seemed like forever. I want to give time back to my family who have been so good. As a player I could only give them the Whit holiday throughout the year. For the six week school holidays, I was always back in pre-season training.

I've always been one for lists and when it came to retiring the positives of me retiring far outweighed the negatives. I didn't like playing the game anymore – and I couldn't then recreate another reason to continue. It wouldn't be being true to myself. I've never minded what anyone has to say about me but the one thing I hope that they do think after meeting me or hearing me speak is that I'm an honest person. And honestly – it was the right time to call it a day.

The way I was feeling could not have been any different to the young lad who was chasing a dream when he was signed up to play for Manchester United back in the late 1980s.

02

Blackstrap Molasses

I was football mad when I was a kid. I grew up on a council estate in Altrincham that was mostly around a generation older than my family in the early days. It was a proud community with people who would take care in the appearance of their houses and gardens. Over time, other families of a similar age moved in and the front doors were always open with kids playing up and down the street.

We'd be out at nine o'clock in the morning and you wouldn't see your mum and dad all day; you might pop back in at dinner time for a pint of Vimto and just to let them know that you were okay but that was it, we were always out with mates. The

neighbourhood changed as we grew up and the older generation sadly passed away and were replaced by younger families.
Still, it was a great childhood.

About two minutes' walk away from our estate was a park.
We'd play football games like 'Wembley' where I'd be Bryan
Robson or Mark Hughes. It was a different world; no-one
would be at home playing on computers or on the phone.

We'd also play 'army'. I'd always be the one who ended up
worse off. I got hit a couple of times in a short space of time
when I was about eight – first time, I was hit with a stone and
got a massive cut on my head. Mum and Dad warned me that
if anything like that happened again I'd be grounded. A couple
of weeks later I got hit again – my head was pissing with blood.
I tried to cover it up and avoid them finding out but when Mum
rinsed my head as I had a bath, blood started to trickle. That
was me done for a couple of weeks. Playing army wasn't the
only time I got myself into trouble – I found myself in hospital
a couple of times. One time was when Mum and Dad got me
a second hand racing bike. The pedals were absolutely lethal.
It was a death trap.

My first proper encounter with Manchester United royalty
came on the municipal golf course. We'd make a few quid
from getting golf balls – we'd hide behind bunkers and over
time we'd know where most of them would end up. There'd be
three of us – one in the bushes waiting for the player to hit his
shot, telling the other two where to run. Later we'd go up to the
players and ask if they'd lost a ball, knowing full well we had it
in our bag. Half of the time we'd probably end up selling the
balls back to the golfers who'd lost them in the first place. We'd
do five for a pound; it wasn't uncommon for us to get 20 quid

between us for the day. There was a brook that ran through the course so we'd have a look in there too – we wanted the white Ultra balls but the holy grail was a Ultra yellow or Ultra pink, or a Golden Bear. Those balls, we wouldn't sell.

I'd get in quite a bit of trouble with Tony Dunne, the former United defender who owned a driving range next to the course. The driving range balls were terrible but we'd always stick our hands through the fence to get as many as we could and then just keep them, for no reason. We didn't even play golf.

So many times I'd get my hands stuck in the fence. My mates would run off, I'd turn around and there was Tony. He was a ferocious fella – with that Irish accent. "What the fuck you doing? Get away and if I see you round here again I'll kick your arse!"

This happened a few times and eventually he gave me two options. "You'll get a kicking or you can collect the golf balls, come around and hit them. That way you'll be collecting them for us and doing some good. But whatever you do, don't put your hands through the fence."

We spent days doing that. They had a soup machine, 10p for the most amazing tasting soup. I never really played golf but it was something to do and I ended up quite friendly with Tony and his son. We were young, but we had a great sense of freedom.

That said, we had boundaries and Dad was always quick to make sure I was doing the right thing. One time I was caught nicking sprouts from an allotment. He gave me a crack and said, "Don't go pinching from these people. If I ever catch you I'll give you a proper hiding." The worst thing was – I hadn't even got sprouts. I'd got the weeds that were on the bottom!

I was always taught never pinch and not to lie. There was one lesson I learned when I had a bet with one of my mates for 50p. He bet me that Liverpool would beat United and I said "No chance." He put 50p on it; Liverpool beat United and the next time I saw him was when I was going to the corner shop. He asked me if I'd got his money and I said no – I got some sweets from the shop instead. He followed me, badgering me for the money. I was in the wrong, I should have given him the money, but I was only a kid. He was goading me until I just smacked him as hard as I could and ran home. Dad was waiting at the door.

He dragged me out of the house and back to the park, telling me to knock on the lad's door and have a fair fight with him. I said "Are you joking?" He was two years older than me! But he wasn't joking. He said I wasn't to come back to the house until I'd done it – you don't hit someone and run. He didn't condone fighting but he hated cowardice even more.

So I did what he asked. We were fighting for about half an hour until he hit me and I fell back, cracking my head against a tree. I ran home crying. Dad answered the door, patted me on the back and said, "That's how you do things." I thought that was the end of it but then he said, "Tomorrow, you know what you have to do. I'll give you 50p, and you're going to knock on his door and give him what you owe him." The next day I did. We were best of mates after that.

That was the school of hard knocks and it could be argued I learned more than in the actual classroom. Having said that, I passed the 11-plus, which surprised everyone, even myself.

Despite my success, we weren't offered the opportunity to go to Altrincham Grammar. It was a real point of principle for

Mum and Dad that I'd passed and I should at least get the choice to go. They had a meeting with the headmistress who said it wasn't a mistake; she said that in their opinion I wasn't clever enough and that I would struggle. My parents argued so much that the headteacher ended up crying. They took it to the government in the end. I kept insisting I didn't want to go but they kept saying that it was the principle. They only decided to drop it once they felt the point had been made. If I'd had gone to the grammar school, I'd have lasted a month. It wasn't for me. They wore blazers – I didn't want that!

My education really suffered when I got to the second year of secondary school. I'd no interest in it, none at all. I was playing a lot of football at the time. Whether right or wrong, if I'd played both days on a weekend, I might get up on a Monday and be black and blue and Dad would sometimes say "Don't bother going to school today." He cared about my education, but he knew. I'm the complete opposite now with my son but he's a lot cleverer than me and financially I'm in a lot better position than my parents were. What my mum and dad did was notice that I had a chance with my football so they literally put everything into making that come true. Dad would say, "Look at where you live now. Do you want a better life than this when you're older?"

That was my desire, my motivation. Mum and Dad had been so unbelievably supportive of me. Dad probably should have been sacked six or seven times as he said he was at work a few times when he was driving me up and down the country with my football. They both worked very hard to provide for me and my brother; they made sure that we were looked after.

Dad, in particular, would be so encouraging. He was an engineer who worked for a company that fixed traffic lights. There was more than just a few occasions that we'd park up on a main road that was near some traffic lights and he'd go and watch me play. He'd be watching from some bushes – just in case there was anyone from his work who passed by!

Thankfully, through my career, I've been able to repay the amazing support my parents gave me. When I moved to Derby County, I was in a position to help Mum and Dad move away. It was the least I could do because they did everything for me – I never went short and they made sure I got everything I needed football-wise. Mind, Dad's methods were sometimes not always the most sane.

Back in the second year of secondary school, I stopped growing. Suddenly, just stopped. Dad started worrying I'd be too short to be a footballer so one day he told the school I had a dentist appointment and took me to a herbal remedy place around the corner. It was just a house! We had a viewing with this specialist who was going to charge £50 at the end of the meeting. I was thinking it was crazy. Dad didn't have £50 for something this ridiculous. The idea was that he'd get a list of all the medicine and pills I'd need that would encourage growth spurts, so we had a meeting and this guy is taking notes. Halfway through, Dad says, "Well have you got any of them here? If you have, we'll buy them from you."

As the guy went into the back, my dad picked up the list he had written, grabbed my hand and we left to go down to the local herbal remedy shop.

The cheapest item on the list was 'Blackstrap Molasses'. If you ever get the opportunity, just give it a brief smell. It is the most

vile thing on the planet, I kid you not. It's for horses' hooves –
it's like a tar that is pasted on them to make them harden. The
tub was like a pot of paint. Every night he would boil some
water, put it in a cup, and mix a dessert spoon full of this stuff
in it. He opened it in the kitchen and it stunk the place out.
When it melts, the smell gets even stronger, and he stood over
me ordering me to drink it. Every sip, I'm gagging. This carried
on for a year. It got to the point where I did it by myself; it never
became nice, but became tolerable.

Over the next year, I shot up about six inches, so of course my
dad swears by it to this day. I bet the only thing it ever did for
me was make my nails grow stronger, or help me grow hooves!
I look back and think what the hell – but it's just an example of
Dad doing every single thing he could think of to try and make
our life better.

From a young age it was always football. My brother, who's 11
years older than me, played non-league and we'd go everywhere
to watch him. He was my hero – I couldn't wait for the end of
the games where I could go to the social club and we could walk
in together – everyone would know I was his brother.

He played non-league football as a centre forward for all of his
career but he could have played much higher up – his temper
sometimes got the better of him – but he didn't enjoy the best
of luck either. I've been to places and watched him score a hat-
trick and then get sent off for hitting an opponent – it would
drive Dad spare.

He was unfortunate once when he was playing for Witton
Albion in the Northern Premier League. Dad had got some
scouts to come down from league teams like Crewe and as we're

sat in the stands, the team news is read out over the tannoy and not only is my brother not in the team, he's not in the squad. Dad went charging down to Stan Allen's office (he was the manager at the time).

"What the fuck are you doing? He's been playing so well – how can you do this – the scouts are here and you're telling me he's not playing at all?!"

"He's gone to hospital!" Stan replied.

Even at that level, my brother was a player that fans loved. They wanted his autograph, and one had been waiting for him as he got into the ground. He signed the autograph and a bit later, in the changing room, he started to feel some pain in his ear. The physio had a look and it was the top of the pen – the only thing I can think happened is that he scratched his ear with the pen and the top came off! The physio tried to get it out but just pushed it further in.

Scouts went to watch him play at Matlock – I didn't go to this, but Dad did – and after just a few minutes he went over horribly and was lying on the floor in a right mess. There were no ambulances, so Dad drove his car on to the pitch, put him in the back and took him to hospital. He'd ripped his medial ligament – just his luck. He liked to play football but he also liked his spare time as well and maybe if anything he was just missing that fine line where dedication becomes sacrifice. I'd say that at least for a while, particularly at an early age, he was more gifted than me – he and Dad would argue otherwise but that's just my opinion.

From my point of view, I knew I wouldn't be able to live with getting to the end of my career and someone coming up and saying, "You should have done much more than you did."

I played every game as if it was my last and I felt like I had to be at the top of my game every time in order to succeed. I'd like to think that a work ethic was around the top of the list of attributes my managers felt I brought.

A lot of that was to do with the knowledge of what my family were doing, the sacrifices they would make. Later on, my brother would also guide me and try to make sure I didn't do the things he did, which was helpful.

Mum and Dad saved up money to buy me a proper pair of football boots. I normally wore Panther Plus – horrible, plastic boots from Woolworths that gave me blisters. Then I signed for Stamford Lads, who were run by a man called Peter Lee. He was a smashing bloke who used to play for Crewe, and is well known around Altrincham for having a window cleaning service. That's when I got my new boots – a pair of Puma Dalglish Silver.

I had my first match coming up and Dad came home one Saturday after he'd been to the bookies – he'd won big, around £30, which was a lot of money then, and he gave me a fiver and said I could spend it on whatever I wanted.

I was football mad so I went down to the local sports shop, Cooper Sports, which is now offices I think, and asked the man there what I could get. I said I already had boots and shin pads. First of all, I got some goalkeeper gloves – the yellow ones with the black bumps – and they were a pound. I got a football that had pictures of the Brazil team on, that was three quid, and I asked the man what I could get with the remaining pound. He said, "Here, this is what you need..."

I went back home buzzing to show Mum and Dad everything I'd bought. First, the football, which I already had two or three of anyway. Then the gloves. Dad said "What do you need them for?" as I played outfield. I said, "For if I want to go in net with me mates." He said, "What else have you got?" and I said, "Give me a second."

I ran upstairs and came back down with shorts on. Dad asked if I'd bought a pair of shorts – I said, "No, no" and pulled them down to reveal a jock strap. Dad grabbed hold of me and took me down to the shop and told the shopkeeper to give me a refund on it!

03

You're Finished

Stamford Lads played on the park of the same name. I was only eight, playing with and against lads who were two years older than me. They played in red and white stripes and black shorts and in that first game, I was a substitute brought on with about ten or 15 minutes to go. I was just mesmerised by the fact I was wearing this football kit which was baggy and way too big for me.

After Stamford Lads I played for a team called Sporting Celtic who played at a place called the Donkey Field. We used to get beaten about 20-0 every week (although one week I remember we only got beat 6-0!). At the end of the season we got the dreaded award for 'most sporting team' because we'd turn up every week and get battered. They were fun times, but Dad insisted that I had to move afterwards. I went to a team called Unicorn who were looked after by someone who was well renowned throughout the world of junior football, a man called Derek Colburn. He looked after the ball boys at Manchester City.

I played in the Timperley Inter-League team which was basically a side comprised of all the best players from the league who would play the best players from the Liverpool League, for example. I was playing well in one of these games that was at Littleton Road – I hadn't signed for a professional club as yet but I was training sometimes with Manchester City at Platt Lane and that was going okay. After the game, I got into the car where Mum and Dad seemed really happy.

Dad said that Brian Kidd had called him into his office and asked him "What colour's your house?"

"Red, it's always been red," was the reply.

"Well what the fuck are you doing with that blue lot then?" Brian said – and that was that. I ended up training at United as a kid, and not City.

At the end of that year I left Unicorn and joined Stretford Vics, another local team who had been successful. Their manager, Jack Fallows, had taken the team out of the Timperley League because it wasn't competitive enough, and put them in the Salford League which was harder but would do us the world of good. I'd been there a year or two with some good players before Jack said he wanted to toughen us up even more, so arranged for a tournament to be played at Salford Boys Club.

Midway through one of the games there was some trouble and we had to make a run for it. Making our way to the minibus was a task in itself as that was getting stones thrown at it. If that wasn't bad enough, they took us back there the following year. 'Character building' they said, "These are things you've got to deal with." We didn't go back for a third year.

We'd play a few tournaments around different places such as Butlins and it was an entertaining time. Jack was great – as was his wife Maureen – he was a scout for Manchester United, and I think still does a bit. They treated you as their own family and were fantastic people to know.

It was a bit of a learning experience all round in the Salford League too. Our captain was a lad called Simon. He was a very good central midfielder who went on to play for FC United. Simon's dad, Pete, didn't get on well with Jack as he felt he was playing his son out of position. We were always used to seeing something happening, whether it was players fighting or whatever, and one week Jack and Pete were having a huge argument on the sidelines.

All of a sudden, Pete took his umbrella out and knocked Jack out! The weird thing was it wasn't a shock, that sort of stuff was what we were used to seeing. Simon, God bless him, was mortified. They made up later on but it goes to show how much it means to the parents who want the best for their kids. I could probably fill a book with the odd stories that happened playing football when I was a kid.

I also played for Trafford Boys and had some experiences that could also be described as character building – some I'll share and some I don't feel are appropriate to.

It was run by school teachers and we used to play dodgeball

at Broad Oak School; we had to play with no tops on, the balls were dead flat and we'd end up with marks all over our body. We were only 12 at this time. There was a fella called Harry who we used to say must have lived in the cupboards at Broad Oak, such was his tendency to just appear randomly. He was only about five foot but he was a lovely, lovely guy. He'd drive the minibus every now and then.

One day, we had a game against Blackpool Borough – he said he had some connections at Blackpool Football Club so would get us tickets for the game.

We were driving down to Blackpool and a couple of the lads were sitting in the seats next to the driver. Harry said, "Here, hold on to the steering wheel a minute while I light me fag." This was while we were doing 70 miles an hour on a dual carriageway! We were oblivious to the danger.

We turned up at the ticket office at Bloomfield Road and Harry introduced himself, saying he had tickets. "No you haven't!" the lady said back to him. "There's nothing here for you!" We went to the Pleasure Beach instead, so it wasn't all bad!

As I approached 14, United imposed the rule that we were not allowed to represent our local sides anymore. All of my experiences playing local football were something I felt would hold me in good stead as I prepared to follow in the footsteps of greatness.

United only had an under-16 team but would play younger lads so it was a good opportunity for me, at 14 or 15, to continue that natural progress. I'd been on the bench as a left winger a few times when Dave Bushell – who was an outstanding influence on my career – intervened.

Dave was naming the team before a game and when he got to number three he said my name. Everyone – including me – started laughing. I said, "Dave, you've made a mistake," and he said, "No, you're playing left back, Danny."

It's not until you get older that you realise people have seen things that you're not aware of at the time – I was only 15, and after that positional change, I went from strength to strength. We'd train at the Cliff on Mondays with Tony Whelan, who is an absolutely lovely bloke; Eric Harrison, whose reputation speaks for itself; Nobby Stiles, Brian Kidd and Paul McGuinness. Some of the best coaches we could possibly have.

Even though I'd had this growth spurt (apparently down to the blackstrap molasses) I was still struggling a bit and I was bullied off the ball; my speed wasn't the advantage it'd once been as people bigger than me were pushing me out of the way.

I used to go in like a crazy fool as I learned the art of defending, diving into challenges. I got a cut on my leg once, and it burned a bit. It didn't get any better after a few days and one evening, sat in front of the fire with my pyjamas on, I told Mum how much it was hurting. She had a look and right from the cut all the way up towards my heart were red marks along my vein lines – poison. It must have been from the artificial pitch.

The doctors sent me to Wythenshawe Hospital and I was on a drip for three or four days. Nobody from United had seen me until Dave Bushell came. He said that he couldn't believe it but I'd shot up in that nine or ten days – he was right. I went on a ridiculous growth spurt over the next year or so. Whether there was any method to Dad's madness with the blackstrap molasses, God only knows, but at least my height wasn't going to hinder me in the future.

United were very good at letting you know where you stood. There were times when people would get released, players you'd known for a few years, but the coaches would say to my dad, "Don't worry, he's doing alright, he's going to be fine." I'd been given my schoolboy forms and was progressing well, before learning of the next step in rather comical fashion.

We were going to a game at Blackpool and obviously I was on the team bus. As always, Dad was coming to the game, and Dave Bushell spotted him driving on the dual carriageway and told him to pull over. He said, "Just wanted to tell you – keep it to yourself – but Danny's going to get an apprenticeship." I still had a long way to go but that was a big reward for my parents and a bit of justification for all the work they'd put in and the sacrifices they'd made. I hadn't made it, but I was on the right road and it was thanks to them that I had any chance at all.

My first year as an apprentice was a disaster, I'm not afraid to admit it. Towards the end of the year – I think, about February time – the club took some of the first and second year apprentices over to South Africa for a couple of games. I was left at home with two other lads and I think if they could have done, the club would probably have released me as I was right at the bottom of the pecking order.

In March, we played a B team game against Preston and I went on an overlapping run from full back – the centre back came across to clear the ball but I got to it first. He followed through his motion and ended up smacking me full on in the knee. It felt like the worst dead leg imaginable – it was so uncomfortable.

The physio ran on. I explained the pain and he thought the same as me, that it was just a dead leg. I got up and as I went to run back into my own half I fell like someone had just absolutely leathered me with a baseball bat in my thigh. Rob Swire helped me walk back to the dressing room. I remember that the facilities were really poor. I was lying on my back in there and all I could see above my head was flypaper dangling down from the ceiling. I asked Rob how long I might expect to be out with a dead leg and he said two weeks or so. I said, "Will I be okay for next weekend?" He said that yeah, I might be, if it sorts itself out quick enough.

The next three or four minutes, the pain starts to become excruciating. Rob called the ambulance as he knew by now it wasn't a dead leg.

When the ambulance came, they gave me morphine as it was all I could do to stop myself from screaming. Rob was brilliant and came with me to hospital – Dad followed, and Mum came with me in the ambulance. The X-rays at the hospital showed that I'd broken my femur. It was absolutely bizarre. Nobody breaks their femur playing football! They plastered from the bottom of my ankle all the way to my thigh.

I got home in time to listen to the first team game on the radio and it happened to be the day of the infamous 3-1 defeat at Southampton where the team changed shirts at half-time from the grey ones to blue and white. The United doctors rung the house and asked if they could come and see me to see if it was okay for me to be at home. When they did, they said I couldn't stay there as our house was too small and I'd have too much trouble tackling the stairs. They took me into a BUPA hotel for two and a half weeks and I kept saying to the nurses that I was sure the plaster had been put on wrong because it was so uncomfortable.

They rang a specialist called Jonathan Noble who came in and used the special electric saw he had to remove the plaster. He took a look at my leg and asked if he could talk to my parents in private – when they came back in they look like they'd seen a ghost.

Jonathan explained that my leg was bent and that it was healing at an angle that not only meant I wouldn't play football again but I wouldn't even be able to walk properly. He said an operation was the only way he could give me any chance of playing again but even then it was 60/40 against. They put three screws through my femur and told me to continue my rehabilitation.

I had a special cast fitted which made sure my leg was straightened. About a month after the operation I was watching my friends having a game in the park when I suddenly declared, "Right, I'm playing!" I was still on crutches at this point, using them to run, when the inevitable happened and I fell over. My left leg went right behind me and I started crying my eyes out. "I'm done. I'm fucking done."

I went home but didn't dare tell Mum and Dad. The next day I went into the club and talked to Dave Fevre, another of the physios.

"Listen Dave, please can I tell you something in confidence? Please don't tell anyone. But I was playing football with my mates…"

"What the fuck were you doing?"

I explained that I'd heard something funny in my leg – noises which I couldn't explain, and I was obviously worried about the screws.

We arranged to go and see Mr Noble who took a look at it and said, "I don't know how – but you doing that has released all your scar tissue. Don't ever do anything like that again but this has ended up working in your favour."

Rehabilitation was very difficult. It was 1996, the year that United got to the FA Cup final against Liverpool. The rest of the young lads went down and I had to sit at home and watch it in the living room with a machine that got me to bend my leg. That was all my summer taken up and I think that's where I developed a strong determination to make sure I was going to get into the first team… it was that determination that played a part in the career I did have, even though I eventually never did make it at United.

I had no means of transport at this time. I started riding my bike to the Cliff, carrying my crutches with me – I was determined to make my legs bigger and stronger than they'd ever been. Recovery took me about six or seven months until I was finally back playing for the B team early on in the '96/97 season at Littleton Road.

What happened in my first game back? I got smashed right on that leg. Back in hospital that night. It turned out that time it WAS a dead leg and to be honest it was the best thing that could have happened to me.

04

School Of United

I suppose it would be fair to say that the generation I was in was probably the last one to encounter the old school experience of a youngster making his way to the first team. It was tough, but then, I'd had 'character-building' experiences already.

Some of the United stories I'll share will sound cruel but it was just the norm, just the education and there were plenty of rewards and so much incentive. As 11 and 12-year-olds we'd go into the Cliff on a Monday and your Nicky Butts and David Beckhams would join in training with us. These guys were incredible, staying afterwards and just continuing to play. Their passion for football and their dedication was unreal.

I was about 11-years-old when I 'megged' one of them in a training session! I felt really bad – I've never meant to do that to anyone in my life. A) because I can't, and B), because, well, I just can't. The first teamers would come for every training session without fail, every time. David Beckham would get tyres, tie them with ropes and hang them from the crossbar of the goal in each top corner. He'd be trying to whip the ball in them, with no pressure from anyone telling him to do it. He was 15 or 16. Great players are blessed with great ability but that wasn't enough; this kind of thing was a special insight for me.

Gary and Phil Neville would come in and tell some of the younger lads to go up on to 'Wembley' (which was the smaller pitch at the top of the hill on the Cliff) just to ping balls at them so they could head it. At the time you think of it as a chore but after time you can see it's that subtle difference; that's what it's all about if you wanted to be at the top level. Gary and Phil continued to do that even when they were established in the first team and that was a real eye opener to the rest of us. It became infectious. If it's good enough for them and they're in the Manchester United first team then surely to God it's good enough for me.

It was a real privilege and we learned so much; I'd like to think that I carried that with me throughout my career and left everything on the pitch. It's clear for all to see by what has happened since that the team with the likes of Neville and Beckham and Scholes were a special generation. For us following them the ambition was to replicate their success – that was certainly how we were motivated by Eric Harrison. Eric's attitude said it all anyway – he had accomplished something great with that team but was not resting on his laurels.

When I started my apprenticeship I was on the bottom rung of the ladder and I was made to feel that way too. We'd be in at nine o'clock, train, do our odd jobs and we'd be lucky if we were out at four. We had to make sure the physio's room and first team dressing room was clean; first team boots, first team showers – everything had to be spotless and if it wasn't, you were in big trouble.

After that two-year apprenticeship you were moved up to the reserve team if they liked you and then you'd be in some afternoons but not all, and you wouldn't have any jobs to do. The progression from there is to the first team room. When you're there, you not only look up to the first team players massively but you appreciate where you've come from and where some of them did too. It also gives you a connection with the apprentices. Could you say that first team players today have a connection with academy players? Times have changed.

When I was an apprentice I'd be cleaning Brian McClair's, Roy Keane's or Terry Cooke's boots. Brian would come up and tell me he remembered when he had to do it. People can't do that now.

A couple of years ago, at Stoke, I asked what the situation was with the boots and who would clean them. I was told, "They don't do that now, you'll have to go up and ask them and then pay them." I thought it was a joke. It's unreal. I used to go home showing off about that – it was a perk of the job for me. My mates would say "You lucky sod." I wasn't bothered if they gave me money, even at Christmas, but at one point Roy Keane would start giving me boots and I was absolutely made up. It was so special to play for the first team wearing the boots that a player of Roy's calibre had. Young lads today would never wear someone else's boots but I would never change what happened – these were great experiences for me.

Brian and Roy were just two of the big characters in that Old Trafford dressing room in the mid '90s. Another was Eric Cantona. I'd just started my apprenticeship when the Selhurst Park incident happened. I was on the park with my mates and it was a freezing cold night; it was live on the radio and I'd taken a pocket radio out to listen. It was unreal – then I saw it later on Match of the Day or Sportsnight. Madness.

Two days later I was walking through Altrincham and seeing people selling t-shirts with stud marks on them saying 'Eric Was Here'. They were selling like hot cakes! He was serving his ban and there was a big furore about it. In order to keep his fitness up, when the first team had games he would come and train with us. I'll never, ever forget that experience.

One time, when we had seven or eight-a-side, I crossed a ball to him and he put it in the back of the net. He looked over at me with that look that he had, put his thumb up and said "Great ball." I could not wait to get home and tell all my mates. Unbelievable.

The club stood by him after what had happened at Palace because he had been such an integral part, the main reason I would say, for United's transformation. To watch him train, his work ethic – he was phenomenal. One of the best players United have ever had. His attention to detail was immaculate. We'd come back in at the Cliff from training or a game and he'd be stood kicking a ball against a wall, trying different things, these were things you learnt simply from observing. The desire which that team had was absolutely amazing.

The characters, I repeat, were extraordinary. Another time,

the apprentices had a couple of weeks off over Christmas but I had to go in for a little bit of treatment on a niggle, it was nothing serious. The first team were playing an 11 v 11 at the Cliff in preparation for a game. I was going to watch it from the canteen but Brian Kidd saw that I was there and asked if I could go and join in. I was shitting myself – I'd never been anywhere near the first team but I wasn't going to say no, so I went and played left back to make the numbers up.

Denis Irwin was playing right back and the pitch was pretty frozen – he went on an overlapping run and touched the ball in front of me. I could have slid in but I didn't want to send him flying; he got past me and crossed the ball in but I don't think anything came of it. Peter Schmeichel came flying out of his goal.

"You little fucking shit! You could have tackled him! Why the fuck aren't you doing it?" he screamed.

I was taken aback – some of the more senior players came up to me and told me to ignore him but it taught me an important lesson. If I was to get the chance to play for the first team again I had to treat it as if it was a normal game.

In a later training session I lobbed Schmeichel – it's fair to say that didn't go down well either! He just wanted to kill me. But he's hands down the best goalkeeper I've ever seen in my life.

Steve Bruce was unbelievable with the young lads. There was an incident with some lads where they sneaked out of digs and got caught. The manager sacked them. I don't know how much of it was scare tactics but Steve went in to see the manager and convinced him to give them another chance. He was great like that. His partner in crime at the back, Gary Pallister, was an exceptional centre half. He looked knackered 99 per cent of the time he was on the pitch but he'd come up against the quickest players and outrun them all the time. I was so fortunate to grow up around these players.

Brian McClair, who'd been so understanding to me earlier, decided he was going to make me the butt of his jokes. He had a column in the club's official magazine, 'Choccy's Diary', and I ended up in it all the time.

One time, the club had just put up fences which separated the Cliff from the River Irwell which ran behind. I was talking to Harold and Frank who worked the gates at the Cliff, two great characters who everyone loved. I asked what was happening with the fences and they said that they were electric fences. "If anyone touches them they'll get electrocuted," they said. "Moreso the dogs – the shock will kill them, we go round with a wheelbarrow and pick them up and dispose of them." I took it all seriously and couldn't wait to tell Brian McClair as I was still his boot boy.

"Choccy, have you heard about these fences? Any dogs touch them and they get electrocuted and die and Frank and Harold go around with a wheelbarrow and pick them up."

Hook, line and sinker. Next thing, that's in Choccy's Diary and everyone's laughing at me. Brian Kidd got me quite a few times, twice which stick out – he sent me once to ask for a 'glass hammer'. Two weeks later he asked me to go and get a 'long weight'. Forty minutes later I'm still stood there and Kiddo says "Have you got it yet?!" "I'm really sorry Kiddo, I can't find one." Everyone was pissing themselves.

The education was tough. When you were second year apprentices, if you did something wrong there'd be a 'court case'.

All you'd hear was the famous noise, "DERR, DERR DERR." I was the first to get one. It was me and Heath Maxon who'd had an argument. The others pumped up the old Umbro balls as hard as possible, wrapped them in a towel, and they'd have what they called a 'Bong Out'. They'd smash the shit out of you with these balls and when they hit you they hurt. I got my nose splatted on my second day as an apprentice. One lad, Gary Bickerton, thought it'd be funny one day to meddle with the bleep test for the second years – they were on about level 13 and he restarted it. He had to go into a bath of piss and have stuff written on him in boot polish and then sit in another bath of piss with ice.

Jon Macken was a lad who seemed to be able to get you anything you wanted. He sold me a coat one time, a brand new coat. He convinced me that I'd love it and I bought it for £30. I wore it to go out that night, put my hand in the pocket and pulled out an ID card – it had belonged to somebody else! He was a second year when we were first years and he'd always be winding us up like that. Rob Trees was their foreman and one day he came in to talk to us and said, "Listen, Macken's been doing your heads in hasn't he? Been winding you up?" We all agreed. He said, "Right, go into his wash bag. There's a full bottle of Dolce and Gabbana aftershave."

To us, at this time, aftershave was still ridiculously expensive. So we got the bottle, all sprayed it on each other and put the empty bottle in the corner waiting for him to come in so he'd be devastated that we used it all. He comes in, and starts absolutely falling about himself laughing – all the second years come in crying with laughter. Something wasn't right. They'd filled the bottle with piss!

Another one was a lad called Johnny Phillips who had a court case. He had to lay down on one of those old school medical beds, stomach down with his blindfolded head hanging over the end. His court case was that five of the lads were stood about six yards away from the bed and they each had a ball that they were going to smash through the bed and hit him in the face with.

First three attempts, nothing happened, fourth one hits him right in the face and knocks him clean out. He's laid out on the floor. Next thing, Eric Harrison walks in, looks about and just steps over Johnny on the floor. Johnny didn't have the best of times. One of his jobs one time was to clean the first team dressing room. He was mopping the first team bed with the same mop he used for the floor. Andy Cole came in and asked him what he was doing – another court case for Johnny.

The manager was always drumming into us the importance of making sure we put ourselves across the right way, that we knew we were representing Manchester United at all times. Rick Wellens had a beard and the manager told him to get rid of it – he said he had to come in the next day clean shaven. Rick comes in the next day and he's not clean shaven so the manager made him shave with nothing but a yellow bic razor.

David Brown was another – I think he was a lad they had big hopes for as he'd been 'poached' from Oldham and they'd had to pay a fairly big fee for him. He had long hair, indie-style like Oasis – the manager told him to get it cut, he came in the next day with his hair the same length so a piece of his hair was taken out to force him to get it cut. "Whether you're in this training ground or not, you're representing Manchester United," he'd always say.

During this time, I still had my dad keeping me on the right road. It'd always be an issue for me, once we finished training, that we had the entire evening and the morning until we could start playing again. I literally could not get enough of playing.

There was a local car park near where we lived – it was floodlit because some people parked there in the evenings. Dad used to drink in a pub opposite called the Bridge, and I'd always know the timings of when he'd leave. The minute he was coming out, I'd just pretend I was sat there doing nothing. One time he left earlier and I was still playing. I thought I'd be in trouble, but just carried on and hoped he hadn't seen me. I got home and for a few minutes I began to believe I'd got away with it until he opened my bedroom door, threw my club blazer in my face and said, "Fuck off. And don't come back."

I went out and was walking around for about three quarters of an hour before going back. He absolutely destroyed me. He didn't lay a finger on me but ripped into me. "Do you know what you're putting at stake here? You're out playing on the concrete, your friends don't care, that's not their career." It gave me a nosebleed. He was right. I didn't do that again while I played for United – though I have to admit that when I was playing for Derby, we'd play on the Saturday and on a Sunday I'd be on the park playing with my mates and I'd even go in goal. Thankfully he never saw me doing that.

Another of the characters at United was, of course, Roy Keane. Even in the early days, he was an inspiration. He always had high standards, demanding the best from himself, which made him such an outstanding captain. There were so many games I saw him almost win by himself. The key one, obviously, was the one in Juventus.

He was very good to me but one time, I'd gone in to training and Jonathan Greening said to me, "Listen, Danny. Roy's after you. He's been looking all over for you – he's gone home now but you've had it in the morning." I asked why and he said someone had rung Diadora on my behalf wanting to get a boot contract – I still don't know to this day who did it. It made me look like I had ideas above my station. I went home, still living with my parents and Mum was asking me what the matter was.

"Roy Keane's after me." I explained what had happened.

"Well, what are you gonna do?"

"I can't leave it until tomorrow. I won't be able to sleep. I can't do that."

I rung the secretary up and asked for Roy's home number. I called but his wife answered. "Sorry to bother you," I said, "Is Roy in?" She told me to call back in 15 minutes – I did and talked to Roy. I said I was really sorry, I'd heard he was looking for me at the training ground. He didn't get angry or anything, I was fully expecting him to rip my head off.

"Danny, you're a good lad. You don't have any arrogance about you. You don't need an agent. You don't need boot deals – you don't need anything like that at your age. I give you your boots." He was brilliant. I explained what had happened and how I was so grateful to him. I actually made my debut for the United first team wearing Roy's Diadora boots, at Barnsley at the end of the '97/98 season.

The first couple of years as an apprentice I'd been trying to keep my head above water. When I got back from my injury I said to myself I had six or seven months to prove myself after what had been a disaster. I went on to play the best football I'd ever played.

I made my FA Youth Cup debut at the end of 1996 and we went on a decent run where we beat Liverpool at Anfield. At the end of that season, I was told I was going to get professional terms. The two lads that had been left behind with me while the others had gone to South Africa had been released, so I considered myself the bottom of the pile. When they said they were giving me a professional contract I was amazed – they said they would send a letter with the details of the offer in. Everyone had been getting a year so that's what I was expecting.

I was sat on the park with my mates a few days later when my mum came up to me.

"Danny you've got the letter."

"Oh great," I said, not unenthusiastic, but I'd expected it.

"You don't understand. They've given you two years!"

"WHAT?!"

In my mind, my recovery and progression from injury had made the difference. The powers that be had studied my dedication and temperament and decided I had the determination to go as far as I possibly could. There were only a couple of people who'd been given two years.

I'd been getting chances in the reserve side towards the end of the '97/98 season and even that was a big deal. To be playing alongside the likes of Jordi Cruyff, Ole Solskjaer, then the bizarre mix of my long time friend Jamie Wood and Brian McClair, whose boots I'd cleaned, was surreal, but nothing quite matched what was an incredible week at the end of that season.

The club gave me the new contract, then the next day I was in the Cliff canteen. Wes Brown had made his first team debut the week before against Leeds at Old Trafford and had done really well; I wasn't jealous as such but envious of wanting that chance. The manager came up to me in the canteen and said, "Listen Danny, the club are away this weekend. There's an appearance I want you to do for us on Saturday."

I was happy, in part, that he thought enough of me to ask but then another side of me thought 'bloody hell' – I really hoped I'd get to be involved. I went downstairs to have a shower and get changed. I had my towel on when there was a knock on the door.

Alex Ferguson popped his head round and said, "Danny forget about that. You're travelling with us to Barnsley." I don't know if there was an appearance or he was just checking to see how I'd react.

The family went down to Barnsley, Mum and Dad getting piss wet through on the last day of the season. I'd been warming up for most of the second half when Brian Kidd pulled me back with 25 minutes to go and said, "Right, you're going on."

Nicky Butt was on the bench and he just looked at me and said, "Danny!" I said, "What?" He just blew a massive rasp-berry at me!

I came on and everything went okay as we won the game – needless to say, that's a shirt that's framed and hung up at home. It was the culmination and reward for a tough personal journey that had begun with the broken femur.

It was a breakthrough, but any sense of complacency I might have had that summer was soon knocked out of me. United had failed to win a trophy in '97/98 and there could be no accusation that the club and Sir Alex Ferguson was taking the situation lightly.

The manager was clearly looking to spend to strengthen his side with Jaap Stam and Jesper Blomqvist signing. Gabriel Batistuta and Patrick Kluivert were linked, but it was Dwight Yorke who was signed instead, from Aston Villa, for a club record fee. Wes Brown was more or less 'promoted' to the first team squad but to be perfectly frank, all that did was underline the fact that his inclusion at the end of the last season had been to do with his own development, and nothing to do with an indicator of how I could expect to be included.

Still, I had hopes I would be involved more, even if that meant just training with them on a regular basis. Maybe that was helped by the fact that, particularly at that time, there was such an inclusive feel in the squad – I became quite close with Jordi Cruyff, maybe on account of the fact that my mum is Spanish. He said to me, "I'll do you a deal. If you learn Spanish over the next year, enough to hold a conversation with me this time next year, I'll pay for you and your family to go on holiday wherever you like." I wasn't earning a lot when he said it – but, me being me, I never did it. I wish I had, looking back!

There wasn't one member of that squad which I was so lucky to grow up with who didn't have time for us. Even Peter Schmeichel, who had been so vicious in that training session, had approached me as I recovered from breaking my femur to say that if there was anything he could do, let him know. A scrawny apprentice being told that by, in my opinion, the best goalkeeper ever! When I did my dead leg, Andy Cole was in the treatment room and asking if I was okay with serious concern. Superstars, but so humble and down to earth.

I began the new season in the reserves and, considering I'd only just started playing for them towards the end of the previous season, it had to be seen as a positive sign of progression. I was at left wing in my first game before moving back to left back behind the new signing Blomqvist – now, I was playing with players who had been in and around the first team on a regular basis so I was trying as best I could to impress them. Jesper was another good one for advice. That's another thing that perhaps goes under the radar when people look at the players the manager signed. Great players, world class players, but almost always first class people too.

The reserve team games were played at Old Trafford, too, so what better incentive?

The only thing better would, of course, be to play there in front of a packed crowd and thankfully that opportunity came in the early part of the '98/99 season in a special match that was organised to commemorate the 40th anniversary of the Munich Disaster. None other than Paul Gascoigne, Laurent Blanc and Jean-Pierre Papin were among the players who comprised our opposition, the Eric Cantona European XI.

Eric was making an emotional return to Old Trafford, so it was packed out. I'd never played in front of a full house there before and I was so excited to do so. It passed by in a bit of a blur – I came on as a substitute for Roy Keane in the second half.

It was only when looking back on the highlights that I realised I'd absolutely smashed into the goalkeeper, Pascal Olmeta. He'd taken the ball out on a dribble and I'd just kept going up the pitch.

It was a fair tackle but you could just see people's reactions – 'what is he doing?' For me, even though it was a testimonial, I was eager to show what I could do.

Afterwards, we all got to keep our shirts and were given ornaments of a boy with a ball at his feet that had actually been bought by Cantona, who ended up playing a half for each side.

The shirt and the ornament still take pride of place in the house. Now my football career has come to an end, I'm able to reflect what a special occasion it was to be a part of. At the age of 19 it was something to savour, though not at the time – right then, it was all about that next step.

I had, and still have, the utmost respect for the coaches and the manager and I worked under the belief that every decision they made or choice they put to me was done with the primary objective of advancing my career, for the better. I never thought there was an ulterior motive; just as I'd been moved from left wing to left back, I felt that when the proposal of a loan move was put to me in September of 1998, it was done with the progression of my career in mind.

As much as I'm sure no-one could have predicted the events of that season for Manchester United – if someone had told me exactly what I was personally about to go through in the next nine months, I'd have thought they were crazy.

05

Banned

I'd only just made baby steps into the reserve team and was looking forward to progressing. Another player might easily have looked at the situation I was in and decided that staying at Manchester United was the right thing, the perfect place for my development. Who could blame them? In 1998, as I've said, their reserve side was as strong as many Premier League sides with the likes of Teddy Sheringham, Andy Cole and Henning Berg making appearances, amongst others.

One September morning, Jim Ryan took me to one side over at Littleton Road and told me about the new connection that the club had established with Royal Antwerp of Belgium.

He explained that United were looking to send players over there and asked if I'd be the first. I had a think about it and spoke to my parents – they felt it would be better for my development, both professionally and personally, in terms of making me grow up. I had no ties. I was still living at home with them. It seemed to be of benefit all round.

I flew out on a Sunday evening. I was to stay at the Waldorf Hotel for the first three months. Being the first lad from England over there, I was a bit cautious heading into training that Monday morning, but to say it was a multi-cultural dressing room would be an understatement. There were at least 14 or 15 different nationalities: Brazilian, Dutch, Belgian, Nigerian, Polish, Macedonian…

Everyone got on incredibly well – at the time, the war and troubles in Kosovo were still very much in the news and I did wonder how the Yugoslavian and Serbians would get on. They didn't know what was going on back home with their families, whether they were safe or not, but I have to say in the squad there was a complete unity. That goes for the club itself too – they are very well supported by a local community absolutely passionate about their team.

Training and playing in a foreign country had its subtle differences from back home. The first thing that struck me was that we all had our own numbered ball – I was number 17, so that was my ball, and it was my responsibility to take it out for training, make sure it didn't get lost, take it back in after training, clean it and put it back in its numbered area.

Eventually, it became a pain in the arse – if someone was doing your head in, you'd find their ball and smack it as hard as you could. Where Antwerp trained was right by their stadium but also next to a forest area, and you'd just blast the ball in there!

The coach at Antwerp was Regi van Acker who was a brilliant guy. Introducing himself to me, he said that Antwerp were a club finding its feet but there was still a pressure and a responsibility as the fans were so passionate. He was right. One of the very first games we played was against local rivals Molenbeek; we lost 1-0, and I gave the decisive penalty away. Hardly the ideal introduction. We lost the next game, at home, and then the following game too – this time, 5-0, in an incredibly bizarre match that we really should have won. We'd played well – we had in all of the games – I couldn't quite figure out why we weren't winning! We got the bus back to the ground after the game and as we approached our ground there were a few fans waiting there. I thought they'd give us commiserations and tell us we were unlucky but even with that in mind I was stunned as I followed the others off the bus. As I got off, I suddenly found I was the target for their disappointment and anger.

"You fucking English bastard – take your passport and fuck off home. We don't want you here. You're shit, you're shit."

Next thing, a woman – who I later realised was Regi's wife – flew in front of me to defend me against the abuse that was being dished out from one guy who was particularly angry.

"Don't speak to him like that – he's a young 19-year-old."

"Yes but he's come from Manchester United, he should be better, he can fuck off, he's shit, we don't want him here."

She got hold of me and dragged me inside the ground. Regi came to see me and apologised. I said I didn't need it – I hadn't gone there to be abused like that. I understood high standards but I wasn't prepared for that kind of extremity – I said in no uncertain terms that I wanted to go home. I couldn't handle it. Regi asked me to sleep on it, and to go for a meal with him and his wife the next day. I agreed but was determined that I wouldn't stay. I spoke to my parents again that night and let it all out.

I went for the meal with Regi. He said, "Please, give me three weeks. If you're not feeling better then I'll pay for your ticket personally and drive you to the airport." I explained my concerns – yes, I understood the pressure, but I was sure that this wasn't the right kind of environment for me to progress my career. After much talking, Regi won me over with his re-assurances and enthusiasm that things would get better. Of course, it almost goes without saying that you believe in someone when they back up what they're saying and things improved almost immediately. Antwerp won their next 15 games in a row.

The turnaround was incredible. After the first couple of wins we came up against a team called Deinze who had a strange little stadium, complete with probably the most bizarre changing rooms I'd ever seen – they had a glass roof. We were really beginning to find our groove as a team and batter our opponents, this particular game was two or three nil. At the end of the match, sat in the dressing room, I could barely comprehend the scale of how things had transformed. To go from such a low to now being completely convinced I should stay was a strange feeling.

Next thing, I hear this loud banging, and wonder what it is. The other lads seem oblivious to it. After a while, we're all looking around, and realise the noise is coming from above. This fella is stood on the roof – the same one who had abused me three weeks previously. He's pointing at me, takes his top off and points to all of his Royal Antwerp tattoos, crying his eyes out. "Sorry Danny, I love you, I love you," he's saying. When we leave the changing rooms he's there waiting for me with tears in his eyes, gives me a massive hug and in his broken English apologises again.

"Antwerp is my life, I was too quick to judge, I didn't understand you had to adapt and that you're so young."

I'd gone from being chastised to almost like a hero in the space of a few weeks – I say that not because of some inflated sense of self worth but because of how they made me feel. They made up songs for me – with my surname, you can appreciate how difficult that must be! – and really got behind me. During the run of games I was scoring goals and playing well. It was a different supporter culture in that they didn't want a photo or autograph, they just wanted to drink with you. The players in the league were all sponsored by bars – so after games, we'd go to one of the player's bars, and of course at the age of 20 I'm loving every minute of it, not having to buy a drink all night.

Christmas came and I was still at the Waldorf. I told the club that I didn't mind staying for the remainder of the season but if I was to do so, I really wanted an apartment – I had a girlfriend at the time and I just wanted a bit more space. The chairman said he'd look into it. He'd also made a promise, when things weren't going so great, that every time we won he'd take us out for a meal on the Monday. Little did he know we'd be winning every week. I'm sure he came to regret that bold act of generosity! We'd have the entire place to ourselves wherever we went and it was great.

One evening we're having one of these meals – all the players are down one side, all the staff and directors down the other end. Before we sit down to eat one of the secretaries calls me over to have a word. He says that they want me to stay after

Christmas but that they can't agree to my request for an apartment. I protested. "Come on, you said it'd be no problem."

Next thing, all of the lights go off.

A woman walks through and grabs me by the hand, puts me on the table and takes my top off. She's got all this cream, puts it all over me, she's doing everything, putting her chest in my face – I was absolutely startled. The lights come back on, the stripper gets off me and the secretary comes over. "Danny, just to let you know – you've got the apartment – we just wanted you down this end so we could do that to you!"

My early days in the apartment, much like Belgium itself, had teething problems. It was the late '90s and mobile phone bills were still prohibitive, particularly for international calls, so I'd make my way to the local phone box whenever I wanted to call home. My girlfriend had come over and decided to stay in while I went to call my mum and dad. The apartment block was coded, so I keyed in to get out and as I'm walking out, this fella I've never seen before is coming in. I went to the phone box with a degree of unease. Something was telling me I had to go back to the apartment.

I'd only been on the phone a minute when I said, "Listen Mum, I've got a gut feeling about something, I just need to go back." There were two flights in the apartment and there was an old couple who lived above us. When I got back in, they'd come downstairs because there'd apparently been a commotion. Of course, they couldn't speak English, so I couldn't really work out what was wrong, but as I walk into my apartment, this fella is there – he'd tried to get in to the old couple's apartment but their door was locked. Mine wasn't. My girlfriend was hiding behind the settee and this odd guy was just wandering around the apartment, so I grabbed a knife to protect myself and marched him out of the apartment block. We walked around five or six yards. I was absolutely shaking as I ordered him not to come back.

Other than that, it was all plain sailing…

United sent Ronnie Wallwork and Jamie Wood out on loan to Antwerp and that was great as I really got on with the pair of them. Jamie, in particular, was one that I'd played with since I was a really young lad. He had a bit of a reputation as a bit of a hard nut – there were a couple of times he got in trouble on the pitch when we were kids!

One afternoon I bumped into the pair of them outside a shop. I went in, and when I came back out there was a big commotion. Jamie had been having an argument with someone who was passing by in a car. This well-built guy gets out of the car and gets up in Jamie's face – Jamie's one of the toughest lads I've ever met so I'm thinking this guy, as big as he is, needs to shut up.

Jamie wound back his right hand and knocked him clean on the floor – the lad jumps up and runs down the street, near enough crying his eyes out, and Jamie runs after him. His car was still running! I've no idea what caused it but one thing that could always be said for Jamie is that he wouldn't back down if someone was confronting him. We knew he'd be backing us up too but I think we all knew that about each other, all of us being so far away from home.

It was never dull. There was a player called Darko Pivaljević who was Antwerp's star striker – he was far superior to the league that we were in. The tunnel that we had in the stadium had bathrooms down the side – before games, Darko would be in there with the other ten of us lining up. Clouds of smoke would come from the bathroom as Darko had a last minute cigarette before the game. Darko would be part of the Yugoslav contingent who'd come out drinking with us – the bars wouldn't have closing times, but would get quiet from about midnight.

One Tuesday night, one of the Macedonian players then decided he'd become the DJ and we stayed there until about 4am. We only went out because we had Wednesday off. As we got in on the Thursday morning, Regi asked me if I'd had a good night on Tuesday, and let me know that he knew I'd been out until four. "Listen," he said. "As long as you keep performing – no problem whatsoever."

I did, and we did as a team, too – we were involved in a promotion race, and although it was unlikely we'd get the top spot, we were confident of qualifying for the extremely complicated Belgian play-offs. A team who were bottom of the league could have such a good run of form over six or seven games and be top of the form table which would earn them a spot in the play-offs. With our great run of results in the second period of the season, we'd already guaranteed our play-off spot come what may. It kept things interesting, anyway – and for us, we wanted to actually win the league.

We had a strong, passionate rivalry with a club called La Louviére. We'd drawn the first league game at their place 1-1 and as we were coming out of the stadium, a few of their fans who had waited for us tried to hit some of our players and then scarpered quick as Antwerp fans, in their hundreds, got wind of what was going to happen and chased them away. When it came to the return game, none of their supporters turned up! Our own supporters had a reputation of their own. I was stripped almost naked after a game, save for pants! Like all clubs, there was an extreme element within the support that seemed to like the violence and some would arrange fights with supporters of other clubs – even clubs from other divisions, when no game was arranged.

Our last game of the regular season was against a team called Turnhout – a team we were also scheduled to play against in the play-offs. Another club in Antwerp had just gone bust so our fans in the away end brought a coffin in with a big sign on it, obviously mocking their local rivals. Next thing, we notice they've opened the coffin up and it's full of beer. Antwerp fans would travel in their thousands and more often than not quadruple the usual gate that clubs were used to accommodating – it was great to play in front of them.

The threat for that atmosphere to spill over into something else happened in the play-offs. We were beaten 2-1 by Turnhout in the first game at our place, despite me scoring the opener. The supporters made a bit of a mess of our own stadium so we had to play the next game against different opposition behind closed doors, which was a bit of an odd experience. It so happened that was against La Louviére, at this non-league ground in the middle of nowhere. Despite the isolated location, there was still the expectation, given the rivalry, that there would be a bit of trouble.

As we drove there, all the houses and businesses had their shutters down as if it was a ghost town. Everything had such a surreal feeling. We're warming up and we can hear loads of Antwerp fans start to sing the songs we're used to hearing. The wind picks up and carries the noise through the surrounding wood, through the ground – as the trees were moving, we could see red dots on the branches, hundreds of Antwerp supporters sat in the trees! It was madness – but it simply underlined how much the club meant to these fans. In return, we loved the fans just as much.

I wasn't to know it at the time but as important as the game was for the supporters, it was about to prove to be one of the most defining days of my own career.

I'll never forget the name of the referee. Amand Ancion. He wore a gold chain, had a fake tan. He was the man. The game was poised at 0-0 going into injury time – one of the Louviére players was put through but was blatantly five or six yards offside. He scored, they won the game and we weren't going to the play-off final.

Obviously, as we're leaving the pitch, there's a lot of tension and animosity in the air. I did something that was rash in the heat of the moment, and it was caught on television (which would strangely work in my favour as it panned out). I'd kicked the advertising hoarding – one of the newer versions where the advert goes around and around for two or three different products – my foot had gone through it, and I couldn't get it back out. I was there for two or three minutes before eventually managing to drag it out. As I walked into the tunnel, all I could see was carnage – I think I've just walked into a warzone. I was so angry from the injustice of the game that I'd ripped my shirt off and tossed it to the ground as I'd entered the tunnel.

Our dressing room was on the right; La Louviére's was on the left, and the referee's was next to ours. There were a few scuffles and then all of a sudden a photographer came out of nowhere and was taking pictures of our lads, but trying to do so in a way that makes our players look like they're the aggressors or perpetrators, when that wasn't the case.

Ronnie and Woody are there and I say we need to get the camera. Next thing, Woody goes through three or four lads and grabs the camera, takes the film out and rips it up. The cameraman disappears and re-appears with a knife – it's mental at this point. He seems to disappear again and we think it's calming down when one of our players goes around kicking the doors in.

I walk to our dressing room and see the referee having an argument with our goalkeeping coach – Ancion's about to hit him, but Ronnie comes in and moves him out of the way. Ronnie pulls his hand back to hit the referee, but then I get hold of Ronnie to stop him – the referee scarpers and gets to his dressing room. Ronnie thanks me but I warn him he might still be in trouble if the referee puts it in his report.

Defeat was the last thing on our mind as we changed and boarded the coach to go back home; thoughts turned to what was likely to be some form of trouble ahead. We got back to the hotel and received a call from Paul Bistio, who was one of the secretaries at the club, and he asks to see us downstairs. Paul's waiting at the machine as two faxes come through; one addressed to Ronnie, and one with my name on it. Less than four hours after the final whistle we've got these pieces of paper that say for the foreseeable future, we've been banned from playing professional football.

None of it made sense. Even if we thought we could at least understand why Ronnie had got into trouble (though it seemed a bit harsh to just ban him without an explanation), even Ronnie himself was asking what I was supposed to have done. Paul was honest – he didn't know, he couldn't tell us, there was just no explanation.

We went back to Manchester to discover it was front page of the Evening News. The problem was that it was a variation of the truth; no, that's being kind, it was a complete and utter lie. Someone had leaked a story and it was complete bull. The Belgian FA went down hard on us – they had to be seen to. Ronnie was banned for life in Belgium and England, and I had received a two year ban in Belgium but a single year in England. I couldn't believe it – all I had to go on were these false rumours that were going around, I was still struggling to understand just what I was supposed to have done.

United were really good with us. The club got their solicitors (one called Scott Duxbury, who became a pretty good friend) to go out there and prepare a defence for us and to be fair to them, they were completely in our corner, they could see it wasn't right. We went to the Glass House, which is essentially the Belgian FA, to see what was happening and hopefully get a proper explanation as to why we'd been banned.

Sir Alex Ferguson came out with us – this was something that was really touching for me. What was he doing? United had just won the Treble, he was preparing his team for the defence of three trophies – yeah, me and Ronnie had played in the first team, but we should have been the last thing on his mind. It showed the measure of the man.

We went into a meeting room and there was a huge table; Sir Alex, the Belgian FA, other United and Antwerp representatives, me and Ronnie at the bottom of the table, and two linesmen and a referee. We're getting the explanation relayed to us through an interpreter and I honestly couldn't believe what I was hearing. The referee was saying that Ronnie grabbed him by the throat and punched him. Then I was supposed to have picked him up and head-butted him. The linesmen backed him up – utter lies. The issue was that Ancion was one of, if not the, best referees in Belgium at the time. Everything he said was gospel, he was their man. When we went back in after they'd had time to assess everything, Ronnie's ban remained the same, but mine had been increased! Two years in England and life in Belgium. I was a complete and utter mess – that might as well have been my career finished.

As you would expect, it was a very stressful time, as we went back and forth to Belgium to try and get everything sorted. I suffered from random nosebleeds which would last for an hour, an hour and a half, I was feeling the pressure so much – no word of a lie. The club did everything they could. In between trips, the manager called us in to his office and offered Ronnie and me new four year contracts. I thought it was incredible, that they were standing by us so much, but naturally when asked if you want to sign something, you say, "I don't know," you need a couple of minutes to think about it. We didn't have agents at the time. The manager said it was okay to go into the canteen, have a drink of tea and a think about it. Ronnie and I just said we'd sign if the other did – so we agreed, and that was that.

Because Ronnie's ban was so much more severe than mine, the club negotiated to get his playing registration back so they could have him playing until they got to the bottom of it. I think because mine was seen as something not quite as bad, they could just hold on. We were playing Liverpool away at the start of the 1999/2000 season – we won 3-2, and Ronnie came on as a substitute. United were struggling with injuries and had to give debuts to Massimo Taibi and Mikael Silvestre, who had literally just signed – I'm not sure it was the manager's usual practice to give players their debut at Anfield! Afterwards, the manager said that he'd have used me if he'd had the chance. Great! I love Ronnie to bits but the only reason I was in this situation was because I was defending him, and he ended up playing before me! It was what it was (and I'm only joking with that, Ronnie!). I was able to keep playing a little bit as the club arranged some in-house games as there couldn't be anything that included a referee or proper opposition.

Meanwhile, this Ancion fella was getting on with business as usual in the top flight of Belgian football and he referees a game that finishes 6-6 – five penalties, four red cards, 12 yellows. Afterwards, he was on national television crying his eyes out. "Danny Higginbotham, Ronnie Wallwork, they're still inside my mind, I still have nightmares about them, they've ruined my life" or words to that effect. The Belgian FA stood up for him but it was clear from his erratic behaviour that things were beginning not to add up.

When it came to the appeal hearing, I had 16 character references that were present – from Antwerp and our opponents and outsiders – and they said that I had done nothing like what the referee was accusing me of. The panel asked him, "How did you recognise it was Danny Higginbotham?" and he said it was because of my shirt number. This was torn apart – the camera footage proved that I had entered the tunnel bare-chested, so all of a sudden, the referee's statements weren't adding up.

A couple of weeks later, he was refereeing another game, it ended 1-0 and the goal is one of the most bizarre to be awarded. Again, he's on television afterwards blaming us, but the head of the referees' association also went on TV and said he needed to get help. The next day, our ban was quashed.

For me, what he did was despicable – though the truth did eventually prevail, the damage that he could have done and what he tried to do to the career of me and Ronnie was an absolute disgrace. It was one of the toughest things I've ever had to do, to sit there and listen to him tell this pack of lies with everyone believing him. For four months he carried it on. Thankfully, no-one who actually knew us thought there was any truth to it. But for many people in a position of influence, those who had the power, they believed it, and it made for a very, very tough time.

Whatever doesn't kill you makes you stronger, right? So I was able to learn from that experience and move forward, appreciating all the opportunities that were to come my way that little bit more.

Since I started working in the media after retirement, you can guarantee that every week, a refereeing decision will be discussed. You can't avoid it. I went on to have other experiences with referees that I'll talk about – thankfully none as bad as I suffered in Belgium – and I think I'm being rational, rather than clouded by my experiences, when I admit I don't have any sympathy for referees.

You're a referee if you want and choose to be, not for any other reason. Nobody said they had to be one. They know what they're doing. The major problem I have with referees is their inconsistency. Everyone makes mistakes – I should know, I made hundreds. When a footballer or a manager makes a mistake during a game, does something they shouldn't have done or says something they shouldn't have said, they're brought to task for it. Referees get demoted but don't have to explain their actions. What's wrong with them coming out 30 minutes or an hour later to explain why they've made certain decisions? Why shouldn't they be made accountable? I've given plenty of referees credit when they make the right decision – some, but not all, are very arrogant.

As it was, I was happy that the Belgian trouble literally just seemed to disappear, back in 1999 – and I was looking forward to being a part of arguably the best squad in British football history.

06

Copacabana

In all honesty, my relationship with Sir Alex Ferguson prior to the incident in Belgium was nothing out of the ordinary. Nothing that would place me in any more special a position than the dozens of other youngsters at the club. Like anyone else, I was in awe of him – particularly as I was a local lad who supported United.

I'm not alone with my recollection about the fact he would always take the time, always remember your name and always ask you how things were. Most of the time you'd just say hello and get on with your jobs.

Once every couple of months he might come downstairs to check on us. He'd go around the entire Cliff and leave marks in certain areas where there was dust and come back to tell us we had an hour and a half to make it spotless. One time he noticed the canteen wasn't up to standard – I think it was Rick Wellens' job – so he gave him a clip with a baseball bat. (I want to be clear here and point out that it was literally just a tap – the bat wasn't used to hurt or threaten us, it was probably just the first thing he found!)

One of my regular jobs was doing the first team drinks and I used to shit myself about making them right. Too weak or too strong? If someone like Peter Schmeichel took a taste and tossed it away, you knew you'd be in trouble afterwards. You had to make sure it was absolutely perfect. Thankfully, it probably only happened once.

The manager really was the perfect example of how to run the club. He was able to have an influence on everything – from the cleaning of the changing rooms and defending two young players in a foreign country to leading his team to European Cup success. Juggling it all at the same time requires a special kind of character and temperament which I'm sure has been said countless times by others anyway. For me, one of the most vital components of his success was the precise amount of coaching he did, or didn't do – his attitude to the delivery of the training was immaculate.

Perhaps my opinion is influenced by the first class environment in which I was educated in the game but I believe a manager is there to manage and a coach is there to coach; all great managers have great assistants.

I have no interest in being a manager but I know that if the thought did ever take me, the last thing I'd want to do is be in the middle of a training session. Maybe on a Thursday or Friday to gauge the feeling and mood around the team, but when you're in the middle of it, it's difficult to assess whether players are taking it seriously or not. Sir Alex had coaches like Brian Kidd and Steve McClaren and Mike Phelan who were tactically excellent, absolutely magnificent coaches. He was able to watch from the periphery and observe the effect the coaching techniques (which he was responsible for implementing) were having on the players. It's far more difficult to see that from the inside.

Brian and Steve in particular were brilliant at the way they welcomed you. If you were a young player, they'd make an extra effort to ensure that the good things you did were highlighted. After such a tough education coming through the ranks, to be given that kind of encouragement when you were around the senior players was absolutely crucial.

The players themselves were just as encouraging. I began to travel with the squad to games. John O'Shea and I went to Sturm Graz with the club for one of the Champions League games. It was a great experience to actually travel in Europe. United won 3-0 and a couple of weeks later played in the Carling Cup against Aston Villa. I was given my full debut in the game, which wasn't that much of a surprise – United, after all, gave younger players the opportunity in the early rounds of the League Cup.

During the game I went up for a header with Dion Dublin, and he caught me on my temple. I've always got on well with him and I know it wasn't malicious – perhaps with my inexperience, I just didn't know how to protect myself going up for such a challenge. Villa got a corner and I looked around at Mark Bosnich (at this time, our goalkeeper, not theirs) and asked him what the score was. I had no idea. I didn't even really know where I was. Bozzy pointed to the physio and told them they needed to come on. I was sat with the physios in the dressing room after the game and I honestly thought I was at home.

We lost that one 3-0 but it wasn't long until I was back in the squad again. When we went down to White Hart Lane, I was so excited my shirt was hung up in the dressing room that I called home to tell my parents. I was on the bench, but even to be a substitute for a Premier League game was so exciting. I didn't get to come on – United had a tough time and lost 3-1, and instead of turning to me on the bench they used Jonathan Greening. The manager was furious afterwards and tore into the players.

"Jonno, what did I tell you to do? What did I say?"

"Take t'touch, get ball out wide and then cross t'ball into t'box gaffer!" replies Jonno in his proper broad Yorkshire accent. Everyone wanted to laugh because of the way he'd delivered the reply but we daren't because of the mood Sir Alex was in.

I was on the bench for the return with Sturm Graz a couple of weeks later – we were two nil up when I came on, then we let in a goal and Bozza had a bit of a dig saying it was down to me. I didn't think so – for me, it was my competitive debut at Old Trafford and nothing could ruin that occasion.

Everything was building nicely for what would prove to be my full debut in the league, against Leicester City that following Saturday.

I was fully expecting that at best, I'd be on the bench, but I was prepared that more than likely I wouldn't be involved. As I walked in, Phil Neville came up to me.

"Danny, you're playing."

"Good one."

"No, seriously, Denis Irwin is injured and you're playing."

I still thought he was taking the piss but Phil was adamant. It wasn't until the team meeting that I realised he was right. All I wanted to do at that moment in time was ring my parents. I knew that in the past, whenever a lad who wasn't local was scheduled to make his debut, the club would make sure his family knew so they could come. I was able to ring them straight after the meeting but they couldn't attend – they got to as many games as they could but just couldn't for this one. It was the only disappointment on what was such a great day, and I was determined I was going to enjoy what had been a childhood dream.

The game kicked off and I wasn't feeling nervous. I got the ball in a challenge with Emile Heskey, and kicked it out by accident, but the referee awarded the throw to us. I'm delighted, Heskey is a formidable character and I feel I've come through that first test well.

Next thing, Roy Keane's yelling over at me, "Danny – what the FUCK you doing? Win the ball and fucking do him!" He didn't want me to hurt him, just lay down a marker for myself. It took me aback that's for sure – but I thought I continued to do alright, and in the second half I played a 60-yard ball through for Ole Gunnar Solskjaer, who couldn't put it away. I even had a shot from about 25 yards but I was never going to take the headlines away from Andy Cole, who scored an absolute belter of an overhead kick to help us on our way to a 2-0 win. With about quarter of an hour left, the occasion got to me and I went down with cramp so had to come off. I got an amazing reception from the fans and it was a great feeling.

We were in the jacuzzi after the game and everyone was having a nice relaxing post-match comedown when Jim Ryan came in and said, "Right lads, everyone's off on Monday." He turned to me and said, "You're not, you're back training with the reserves."

It might have been just in case I was getting ideas above my station but there was no chance of me doing that again – it was just a nice treat to be involved. I could look at the situation for the Leicester game and say that with Phil Neville and Mikael Silvestre capable of playing left back, and David May and Henning Berg on the bench, the decision to play me was a huge vote of confidence, but the truth was at the time I never saw it like that.

Sure enough I was back in the reserves that same week, first for a game at Newcastle and then at home to Everton. As well as I'd done against Leicester, people were probably keeping an eye on me to see how I reacted. We played in the morning as England were playing Scotland in the Euro 2000 qualifying play-offs, and I don't think I did myself justice. It was difficult, at first, to come to terms with being involved with the first team and then playing for the reserves at Gigg Lane, home of Bury, but it was something I got used to.

After the international break, I was given a reminder that I wasn't first choice even with Denis Irwin still injured as I travelled with the squad to Derby but wasn't even on the bench. Denis travelled too and explained that he thought I'd done well but had to be patient – words I agreed with and took on board. I wasn't getting ahead of myself at all but at the same time I never gave any thought to anything other than being a footballer. That's not because I felt as if I was this incredible star or anything like that. I really would have been up shit creek if I'd not been a footballer – I didn't do well at school, it'd only been football from the age of 13 or 14. It wasn't arrogance when I said I'd be a footballer when people asked me what I would be, it was simply my single-mindedness. Even at the age of 19 or 20, it can be a critical time when so many players fall away from the game, but that never entered my head. All I thought about was the game on Saturday.

The quality of that team that were fresh from winning the European Cup ensured that I didn't feel nervous making those first appearances as a squad member. It was different to the debut I'd made in 1998 against Barnsley. Gary Neville once said that he felt he had coasted or underperformed throughout the 1999/2000 season but as far as I was concerned that was an unbelievable squad at the very peak of their powers. If he felt he was underperforming it wasn't something I noticed. Maybe what he meant was that he was able to look a lot better in that team because of the sheer quality around the pitch; either way, that's certainly something I was able to identify with. I felt like I looked a much better player alongside the likes of Jaap Stam and Roy Keane. What a squad, jam-packed with leaders. There were so many options. Everyone wanted the ball, no matter who was in that team. I didn't have to do much defending on my full league debut but I knew that by getting a spot in this incredible team that I had earned it – it's not lucky to play for Manchester United. It's an absolute joy – football is made simple for you.

My next involvement with the squad was travelling to Tokyo as United prepared to become the first ever English club to become 'World Champions' by virtue of winning the Intercontinental Cup against Palmeiras of Brazil. I'd never been anywhere like that in my life and it was just an honour to be part of a Manchester United team travelling to compete for this prestigious title. The journey was a bit of a nightmare, and when we got there I was told not to sleep so I could try and come to terms with the jetlag.

The set-up in Tokyo was luxurious – the hotel was class, everything seemed magnificent. The lads said that to stay awake I should get a massage – it sounded like a good idea. I called down and asked for a masseur. This woman came up, she must have been about 80, and I'm not kidding, she absolutely battered me. Standing on my back, hitting me in all these places, ripping my hands behind my back, I just wanted it to stop – those fuckers knew exactly what was coming to me, and one thing's for sure, I didn't get any sleep. I was black and blue. I had pain in places I didn't know existed.

Later on we went to an amusement park. There was one of those rides that shoots right up into the sky. I'm shit-scared of heights but because the other players went on I couldn't show my fear. I was petrified and so relieved when it came back down. Then another bunch of players said they wanted a go – I had to go on again. I went on it three times in all and I was too worried to say anything!

The game itself was surrounded in a blaze of publicity and went according to plan for United. Roy scored the winner, and Ryan Giggs was awarded the man of the match – his prize was a Toyota car, quite an upgrade from the usual bottle of champagne. In all honesty, I think Mark Bosnich was the best player on the day, he was unbelievable.

It was a big thing, of course, but it was difficult to really feel a part of it when I hadn't played. I'd got a medal but couldn't really feel as if I'd earned it. That was a feeling that would follow me around later on, too.

Shortly after the trip to Tokyo, Sir Alex was leading United into unknown territory in the inaugural World Club Championships in Brazil, to be held exclusively in the famous Maracana. Once again, I was included in the squad.

Just as back in the 1950s, the club faced controversy by locking horns with the FA – this time around, the decision was taken by all parties that United wouldn't defend the FA Cup. There was a suggestion that the club could field a reserve side in the FA Cup while taking a strong side to Brazil but for whatever reason that didn't happen.

Just like when we went to Tokyo, I'd do anything to become an accepted member of the squad. When we were in the airport departures lounge, one of the electronic shops was selling the first DVD players so a few of the players bought them – at around £750, they were really expensive. Maybe I was carried away by seeing the likes of Gary Neville and David Beckham buying them but I felt like I had to get one!

Brazil was fantastic. Every morning we'd go for a walk along the Copacabana and very early on we realised that the media pressure on Beckham was huge – they were after him in a big way. On one of these walks, a girl came up to him and asked him for his autograph.

David, being as courteous as he always was, agreed, and as he was about to sign, a photographer came out of nowhere. The girl tried to do something like kiss him, but then Andy Cole got wind of it and pushed the photographer out of the way.

It was absolutely disgusting to see his good nature taken advantage of in such a way and Andy went suitably mental at them. That was just a small insight into what David's life must have been like on a regular basis. That was an incident that was clearly intended to be blown out of all proportion, it was purely a set-up.

We'd had a good week before the first game to prepare and acclimatise. One afternoon, we were relaxing by the pool. All of the squad were there except for Roy Keane and Nicky Butt. Near the hotel was a big mountain and we'd been told in no uncertain terms that we were not to take part in any of the leisure activities on offer. Some of the players ignored that instruction and said they were going to go hand-gliding.

Soon after, we saw a couple of gliders coming down with instructors. As they're getting closer, we're trying to make out who they are. Next thing, out of nowhere, Sir Alex comes to sit with us. That was something that rarely happened. He'd picked today of all days to have a bit of a chat!

As the gliders get towards the hotel we start to hear the shouts of 'Alright lads, alright lads!' and look up to see one of the lads waving. Luckily we can't really make out who it is but Ferguson looks and he's asking questions. We make out it's a couple of people we've got to know out there. Next minute, another comes by, shouting to get our attention again. Again, we make our excuses and – I think – we all get away with it. If Sir Alex, Roy or Nicky are reading – sorry!

The tournament itself didn't quite go the way the club wanted it to. There was more controversy in the first game when Beckham was sent off for a situation similar to the one in the World Cup. Then, in the next game, we were beaten by Corinthians which meant we couldn't progress.

The remaining game was against South Melbourne, which effectively meant nothing, but fair play to the manager who must have seen it as an opportunity to reward all the young players who'd travelled. It had been mentioned in the morning newspapers that a few of us would play and my name was among those named; we had a meeting on the morning of the game and the manager stands up in front of us.

"Listen lads, the trip has been a success in terms of us actually getting here and participating but obviously on the pitch it hasn't been the same. Some of you would have read in the papers that I'll be giving some of the younger players a game today, and yes, I am. I'm also sure that you've read that there's no pressure on you today and that you can just go out and enjoy yourselves. I can guarantee you now that is fucking bullshit. You young lads are going to play, and there is pressure on you. Go out and enjoy yourself but you've got to prove you can play for Manchester United – forget what it says in the newspaper, that's bollocks. There's always pressure when you're represent-ing Manchester United and I not only expect to see a good performance but I expect you to beat South Melbourne."

I was half expecting him to say we could enjoy and express ourselves; I wasn't prepared for the intensity and I think I could speak for the other lads on that too. As we're walking out, Ryan Giggs says to us, 'Good luck lads'. Yeah, thanks for that! As it turns out, the game was brilliant. We won 2-0 with early goals from Quinton Fortune but the conditions were incredible – we weighed ourselves before the game and we cut our shirts to give ourselves more air. We weighed ourselves again at half-time and lost about two or three kilos of fluid – it was mind boggling.

I've always tried to keep looking forward and never rest on my laurels so there are so many things that I'm not sure I fully appreciated at the time. Now, sitting down to write this, I am able to say that I played at the Maracana Stadium. I played with all those great players and that was a great feeling but to know them, too, was a real honour.

My involvement for the rest of the season was largely with the reserve team and as well as the established stars who I've already mentioned, there was a number of players like Michael Twiss, Alex Notman and Bojan Djordjic who were all talented youngsters but not really getting a chance in the first team. One valuable lesson that I'd now learned from my brief flirtations with the first team was that as a player you always had to conduct yourself well and in a professional manner (and this was something I carried through with me for the rest of my career).

I remember my debut for the reserves, when Jim Ryan and Brian McClair had a hell of an argument. They were the best of friends normally but this one game against Sheffield Wednesday, they were really going at each other. We were battering Wednesday and Choccy was in midfield but at half-time he and Jim had a full-on row. I was taken aback by the intensity just for a reserve game but that was just how it was when you pulled on that shirt. It's not only how you conduct yourself but how you're observed by others; I'd learned that, after all, by observing. The professionalism and character showed by some of the senior players was incredible – they had to maintain a certain level because when they were called upon to play in the first team they were representing the best team in the country.

United were defeated by Real Madrid in the Champions League but made up for that by winning the Premier League very early on the next weekend against Southampton. There were four league games left and that meant there was going to be an opportunity for some of the fringe players.

I came on in a televised game against Graham Taylor's Watford side when we were losing 1-0. We ended up winning 3-2 – Jordi scored a late winner. It was a gorgeous day at Vicarage Road and as we were walking off, Nicky Butt says "Look at you, you'll be able to tell all your mates that you came on when we were losing and we ended up winning."

For me, to be involved in these occasions was absolutely incredible – it's almost impossible for me to articulate what it meant to me. That association with United never leaves you. It's normally the first thing people ask me when they ask about my career, even though I played more than 400 times elsewhere! That's just the power of the club.

My last game was against Aston Villa but that in itself had a bit of a back story. Early on in the last week of the season, there was a squad due to go out and play against Antwerp, and Ronnie and I were asked to go whereas a couple of other fringe players like Jonno were kept behind. I thought the logical explanation was that the squad for the final game had been selected and I wasn't part of it. Fine, I was a bit disappointed, but it wasn't to be. We went out to Antwerp and played on the Friday – it was fantastic as I got the opportunity to say goodbye to the supporters. Throughout that season and particularly in the early days when we were in the spotlight, the supporters had been incredible – apparently they'd had banners made up saying "Ronnie and Danny, you'll never walk alone" and waved them at games. They'd really fought our corner and got behind us which was appreciated – to acknowledge that was a very emotional experience.

After the game, Regi came on to the pitch and asked me to go with him to the stand with the most vocal supporters. He gave a sign to them and they lit loads of flares and began singing my chant – it was obviously pre-planned and it was amazing. "Botty," said Regi, as that was my nickname to him, "You come back here next year, come back on loan. Look at these supporters. Look how much you mean to them, they love you."

That evening, with it being the end of the season, I said to a few of the lads, "Let's go out." Obviously I was friendly with a lot of the Antwerp lads and they knew where to go so out we went, had a great time and got absolutely plastered. No trouble at all, we were well looked after and got back to bed at about 4 o'clock – knowing full well we'd have to be up at eight to get the flight back to Manchester. I was still worse for wear – in fact, probably still drunk – getting on the plane, and when we got back to Manchester one of the coaches says, "Ronnie, Danny – you're meeting up with the squad this afternoon." Nice way to drop a bombshell!

We got to the team hotel and the next morning, I'm sat at the back of the team meeting thinking at best I'll be named on the bench because there might have been a couple of injuries. I'm named at left back. "Shit," I'm thinking. I couldn't believe that less than 48 hours earlier I'd not only played but got hammered. Thankfully, the manager's thinking was that Ronnie and I would get a half each and that's how it panned out. I was blowing out of my backside quite a lot in that first half, I don't mind admitting it – I came off at half-time and unbeknown to me that was my last appearance for Manchester United.

My thoughts for the future hadn't really taken shape if I'm being honest. I didn't think I'd played my last game but I was very mindful not to be one of these players who outstayed their welcome.

With all respect to those who do, I couldn't see myself as a player who stayed to the age of 22 or 23, played one or two first team games and then 200 reserve games. Having signed the four year deal at the start of the season I'd said to myself that I'd give it one more season, another year, and if at the age of 22 I wasn't at least a regular in the first team I'd look at going elsewhere.

It'd been something of a whirlwind year. Not only had the manager given me a chance to play for the club I loved, but his personal intervention had probably saved my career. To him, who was I? Someone minor. He had bigger fish to fry. He may well have seen what he did as part of his job but it was something that my family and I have been eternally grateful for – and for me, the future was all about making the most of the opportunity that had been given back to me.

07

Ram Raid

During the summer of 2000, I was at home when I received a call from Scott Duxbury, the solicitor who had been so helpful during the Antwerp saga. It was about 10 o'clock, I was having breakfast and I was still living at my parents, although they were on holiday at the time. It was unusual to hear from Scott – of course we'd had regular contact but the trouble in Belgium was long gone.

"Got something to tell you but please don't say anything."

"Yeah of course, go on."

"I was in the office earlier and there'd been a phone call come through about an offer from Derby County that had been accepted. Alex Ferguson will call you in the next couple of hours, but I just wanted to prepare you."

I was genuinely shocked. I hadn't given any thought to anything other than preparing for the new season at United and hoping a good pre-season might get me into the first team picture. Yes, I'd accepted that in a year's time, I might have to look elsewhere, but moving now was not in my plans at all. Sure enough, two hours later, Sir Alex called. Again, I'd had an increased communication with him over the last two months but it was strange for him to be calling me at my home. We'd never had what I would call such a personal dialogue but fortunately for me I knew what was coming.

"Hi Danny, how are you, how's your summer going?"

"Everything's good here Gaffer."

"We've had an offer from Derby – it's a good offer and we've accepted but one thing I'm going to say is that your time isn't done at this football club. You do not have to leave. You had a good year. But you have Denis Irwin, Mikael Silvestre and Phil Neville in front of you in the pecking order…"

To me, that was a message that it was better if I left. If a manager doesn't want to sell you, you wouldn't even hear of the offer – well, that's how it was then. Obviously today, with agents, you'd hear well in advance. I didn't. I also felt that if the manager felt I should stay, he would have told me about the Derby bid but then said he 100 per cent didn't want me to leave. Fair play to him – he was honest, and left it up to me. He said he'd give me 24 hours and then call me the next day.

I had a good think and called my parents. When I considered the cold hard facts, he'd effectively said my opportunities would be limited. I'm not someone who would pull the wool over my own eyes and the manager had mapped out how the year would unfold for me at United.

Innocent days: Left: Enjoying some early silverware in a five-a-side tournament. Far left: On tour in Scotland with Stretford Vics in the late '80s. I'm on the back row, second from the left

United dreams: Getting my hands on the FA Cup and (right) at the School Of Excellence. The smile says it all – I was at my happiest playing football

Famous faces: Receiving a trophy from Sir Alex Ferguson as one of the Under-11s youth squad and (above) posing for a picture with Nobby Stiles

Cream of the crop: With the Manchester United youth squad in Northern Ireland (above) for the 1995 Milk Cup

Best education in the game: The coaching team at United was second to none. I'm on the back row next to Paul McGuinness. Eric Harrison is back row, far right

Young guns: We were tough to beat when we played in the Lancashire League for United

ROYAL ANTWERP FOOTBALL CLUB • SEIZOEN 1998-'99

Euro adventure: A Royal Antwerp team picture. I'm front row, second left. Ronnie Wallwork and Jamie Wood are behind me.
Left: In action for Antwerp against Turnhout in December, 1998

Crazy days: The Antwerp culture was a real eye-opener. This is the band welcoming the team on to the pitch

Big in Japan: In Tokyo after United had won the Intercontinental Cup. Denis Irwin – the man whose left back place I was competing for – is holding the trophy. Also pictured are Jaap Stam, Gary Neville and Ronnie Wallwork. I'm pictured far right – holding the man of the match trophy!

Glory daze: I'll never forget playing for Manchester United at Old Trafford. I made my full league debut against Leicester in November, 1999

Moving on: I had to adjust to a different way of playing when I joined Derby County in 2000 – but I enjoyed the challenge of regular first team football

Master class: Back on home ground, keeping a close eye on the legendary Roy Keane in December, 2001. I was on a real learning curve at Derby

Pressure spot: When I took the penalty off Fabrizio Ravanelli against Bolton, I knew I had to score – thankfully I did. Left: The sheer relief of survival! With Chris Riggott and Rory at Old Trafford

Gord life: A spot of training with my new boss Gordon Strachan. He was a great manager and we enjoyed some interesting times at Southampton

Tough test: I came up against some top strikers, including Newcastle's Alan Shearer

Highs and lows: (Above) A last minute equaliser against Crystal Palace in May, 2005 gave us hope of staying up – but it wasn't to be. Just two years earlier we had recorded our highest finish in the Premier League

Changing times: Battling with Wayne Rooney in a 3-0 defeat at Old Trafford in December, 2004 (below). The return league game was at St. Mary's on the final day of the season – we lost 2-1 and were relegated. Right: Back in the Championship. It wasn't long before I was on the move again

First love: It was an inspired decision to join Stoke – I rediscovered my passion for the game. Top: A goal against Colchester in April, 2007. Middle: True team spirit. Right: Missing out on the play-offs was hard to take but being named captain (left) by Tony Pulis was a fantastic honour

In accepting the bid from Derby County, I'm certain the manager was still acting in my best interests and assessed everything for the good of my career – whether it would be a good club for me to continue to progress; whether I would develop better there, and whether they would look after me. United, under Sir Alex, had always been good at looking after young players even after they'd left because no matter where you go and who you play for, the association and tag of being a Manchester United youngster never leaves you. For a player to leave the club and still play at a high level is another feather in the cap of a successful youth system and United are more prolific than any other.

And, again, I felt the manager had gone above and beyond what he needed to do – did he need to call me personally at my house? He could have got a coach to do it, or a reserve team manager. I'd like to think that was because of the way I'd conducted myself at the club. Yes, there had been Belgium, but I was hardly to blame for that and I felt I'd not been a minute's trouble at the club since I'd been there from the age of nine. When he called me back the next day, I informed him it would be best for me to move on. We discussed agents and he offered to help but I'd just got one – little did I know, but that turned out to be a bad call.

Jim Smith was Derby manager at the time and my agent and I flew out to his place in Marbella. We discussed the future and Derby's plans and he offered me a massive wage increase to what I'd been on at United. Jim said, "You can use us and we can use you. We hope you're going to be a good player for us, and you can use us as a stepping stone to further your career."

After the meeting I asked my agent's thoughts and he told me he thought it was a good move – Derby were a good, established Premier League club and if I waited that extra year it might be lower division clubs who would be looking at me. Football can be all about timing and when I thought about it, I felt that the time had come for me to leave United and join Derby. We flew back, I spoke to Mum and Dad and concluded I was going to sign for them. The agent was all frills – we grew up on a council estate (and we were still living there) and he hired this great big bloody Rolls Royce to take my mum and dad to Derby. They were so embarrassed to get in. It was probably worth more than the house itself.

There was nothing 'flash' about Derby County and I don't mean that in a derogatory way. The first day of pre-season training was a world away from my usual experiences at Manchester United.

It was all running for the first couple of days, led by Steve Round, who of course would later become the assistant at United. The old training ground was called Rainsway – it was only a small building, next to the pitch and a small bowling green type of area where they ran five-a-sides on a Friday. Next to that, there was an indoor astro turf.

On the first day, we did a bleep test – the second, we did a 'yo yo' test in the indoor area, which is similar to the bleep test but more continuous runnings. After that, we came outside, and the nearest area was the bowling green – I laid down on the grass and I was heaving for fun. Nothing coming out except for bile. My head was spinning, I was so dizzy – I opened my eyes and Steve was stood over me, asking me if I'm alright. "Fucking hell – I'm fine, but I've never done anything like this."

"Danny let me tell you, the club you've come from and the club you've come to – we're in the same division but we are worlds apart. We spend 90 per cent of the game chasing the ball and United spend that time with it – you need to be fit when you're playing for Derby because most of the time you'll be chasing."

We went out for a training camp in La Manga – the lads were allowed to take their partners, but I went alone. The apartments we stayed in were two storey and we were to stay in small groups. I'd only been with the club a couple of days before I'd earned the nickname 'Brains' because I was supposedly thick. I didn't help my cause. I was staying with Seth Johnson, who gave me the nickname, Dean Sturridge and Craig Burley. Knowing there was likely to be some golf, even though I hated it, I'd brought my mate's clubs along as I desperately wanted to make a good first impression and fit in. One of the first things I did was knock over a vase – it was about three foot high, and I've absolutely shattered it by knocking it with my golf clubs, completely by accident. Not exactly brainless, but, doing my early reputation no favours!

It was a training camp but we'd go out and get pissed every night, working that bit harder in the morning to shake it off. We'd all get drunk and Craig was no different. His front two teeth were false, and randomly throughout the night he'd take them out and drop them in someone's drink. God knows how many he lost!

We played a drinking game called 'Peanuts' and if someone had any peanuts by their drink you were allowed to smash them. I was sat by Craig one night and I kept doing it for about half an hour – suddenly he just snapped and said in a thick Scottish accent, "I've fucking had enough of you" and grabbed me in a headlock! No word of a lie, he's kept me in this headlock for about an hour, sat down, walking around. Being so young and fairly insecure at this new club with these new players, I wasn't quite sure what to think. Later on, Craig got so drunk that we had to put him to bed.

I'm sharing a room with him so the next morning I go in and ask him, "Are you alright? Do you like me or not? You had me in a headlock all last night!" He said something to me which was to ring true wherever I went afterwards. "In football, if you're liked, people will piss around and have a joke with you. If we didn't, we'd leave you to one side." It was an affection and team spirit that ran through the club and I feel certain that it was this quality that kept us up in the Premier League in the 2000/2001 season.

Neither Derby or myself started the season in any great form. We drew with Southampton in the first game of the season and although we narrowly lost against Newcastle United in the second, I felt I did quite well against Nobby Solano and that I was getting used to life at Derby. Next game, we were at Goodison Park and I came up against Niclas Alexandersson – we were 2-0 down at half-time and I got dragged off, rightly so as well. He destroyed me, well and truly took me to the cleaners. It was one of the few games in my career where I actually wanted to come off.

Derby had paid a fair amount of money for me – £2m – but that didn't mean I was undroppable and I was out for a few games after that. It took a while for me to get back in. With the team themselves not doing so great, I always had a chance of getting back in and I played in a creditable draw against a strong Leeds United team. We were losing 1-0 when a goal from the substitute, Georgi Kinkladze, earned us a point. Georgi, honestly, had the potential to be one of the greatest players I ever played with – he was such an enigma. He had all the ability, it was just if he wanted it… he had all the tools necessary to play for a Barcelona or a Real Madrid. His goal in this game was proof of that – ball gets thrown to him, he nutmegs Ian Harte, takes on Lucas Radebe and puts it in. Maybe he was in his comfort zone but if he'd had the same desire he seemed to have when he was at Man City he would have been one of the real top players.

As decent a result as that was, we lost our next four games, shipping four goals to Villa and Liverpool. After an unconvincing home draw with West Ham, Jim Smith decided he was going to switch to three at the back. I'd played on and off but I wasn't a guaranteed starter. In the midweek after the West Ham game, I played for the reserves against Tottenham in a three man defence. I had a stormer of a game – probably my best of the season and definitely the best I'd had since I'd joined the club.

We travelled to Arsenal and because we were a close-knit squad, loads of the lads had seen the reserve game and were giving me praise for my performance, saying the formation had suited me. It was probably the players who influenced Jim's decision – I played on the left hand side of a three again at Highbury and we got a very well deserved 0-0 draw. Things were beginning to look up, though it took me a while to get back in on a permanent basis. Derby registered their first win of the season the week after the Arsenal result, with a 2-0 victory over Bradford, which was the first of five wins in nine games.

I was on a real learning curve and I have to admit that for around the six or seven months straight after signing for Derby, I let the money I was earning go to my head a little bit. I bought an Evo VI, and one Tuesday night after training we went for a night out in Birmingham. I was driving, a few of us were going and the lads were egging me on down the A50 to see how fast I could get the car going. I was hammering it, doing something like 152mph at one point. It was stupid, reckless.

A Mondeo started following me, and when the lights started flashing, I realised it was an unmarked car. I got off at the next turn-off, and stopped on a roundabout. No-one even had their seatbelts on. The police came and knocked on the window and asked if I knew how fast I was going. 'About 120?' I reply, before being asked to step outside the car.

Instant jail for me, I'm thinking, as I'm led to the police car. They showed me the footage of me on 152. They were almost playing 'good cop, bad cop' – one of them telling me they could take me to jail right now. Then they recognised who I was and that meant it could go one of two ways, as I was driving through the Nottingham area at the time.

"It's your lucky day," they say to my surprise. "We're both Derby fans, now get out and don't let us ever see you doing anything like that again."

The following day I was driving to Manchester to meet my agent. I was on the M56 and it was belting it down. All of a sudden, the car started to aquaplane, and although I wasn't doing anywhere near 150mph this time, I wasn't going as slow as I should have been. The car spun and turned towards the barriers. 'I'm dead, I'm dead, I'm dead', is all I could think, but the car hit the barrier and actually spun me around towards the central reservation instead. The airbag came out and softened the blow, and I emerged from the crushed car with little more than a cut lip. I was sat in the central reservation and a couple stopped on the hard shoulder. I was white, they were whiter than I was, asking 'How the hell have you just walked away from that?' I couldn't answer. What I did know is that it was a warning. Slow down.

From January onwards, I began to play more regularly in my new position but the difficult start and a run of only two wins in 11 after New Year's Day meant we were always involved in a relegation scrap. We beat Leicester, but then lost at Bradford and then at home to Arsenal in a tight game. Despite this, I won the man of the match award, which was a real big thing for me as I was still trying to establish myself as first choice. The coming week we were going to be taking on United at Old Trafford. That was a game I did not want to miss. Out of the two games left, we'd put ourselves in a position where one win would guarantee our safety, but we were looking ahead to the home game against Ipswich on the final day rather than Old Trafford as a place where we might pick up the necessary points.

We travelled over to Mottram Hall early on the Friday before the game, trained there and stayed overnight. All of the signs had pointed to me playing, so I was happy – we'd settled on a 3-5-2 formation and that's what we'd been playing most of the season, so I was well prepared.

Saturday morning, there's a bit of a commotion as we're having breakfast. Jim Smith and the physio Neil Sillett (son of John, who managed Coventry) are having this debate because

Jim has apparently seen a formation of DUCKS in the gardens of the hotel through the window and believes it's a sign. It was a bizarre 3-4-3 formation and, remembering the potency of that United team at the time, setting up in such a way at Old Trafford was surely asking for trouble.

Taribo West had been part of the squad that season and I can't remember why, but he wasn't playing that day. Taribo was an eccentric, religious man – his first game for us had been a cup game against Fulham and he insisted that we all said a prayer before the game. We all stood around him as he was screaming and shouting. We didn't know what to make of it, we'd never been used to anything like that. It was bizarre, a bit like Taribo's time at Pride Park. On occasions, he was phenomenal, the player we'd seen at Inter Milan; other times he wouldn't really play well or even turn up at all. You never knew what to expect. I remember Chris Riggott once stood up to him at half-time in a game and Taribo had said to him, "Talk to me like that again and I will kill you." For whatever reason, he wasn't there at Mottram but as we're walking on to the bus to go to Old Trafford, I've got a book in my hand. Jim Smith says to me, "What's that Danny? I hope it's Taribo's bible, because we're going to fucking need it today!"

We really were going to need all our prayers – United had just won their third title in a row, it was their last home game of the season and it was going to be a big celebration. Taribo wasn't the only character we had – Paul Boertien was another. He was a left wing back, but before games, he'd sit and count toes. It was weird. Georgi sat next to him and it drove him mad. "I cannot sit next to this man, he talks to himself and he counts his toes!" he'd say. We had character in spades and we were going to need to call on all of it if we wanted to even get a point from United.

We got to Old Trafford and started our warm-up and then we heard the United team – it wasn't the strongest they could put together, but featured Barthez, Neville, Johnsen, Irwin, Beckham, Butt, Sheringham, Cole with Giggs on the bench. That was still strong enough to win any game they wanted in the league, and we still felt like lambs to the slaughter. We gave them a guard of honour as a sign of respect and the game started as you'd expect – it's backs to the wall stuff. I'm not certain if the record stands to this day but, at the time, it was the game that featured the most blocked shots from one side in a single game in the Premier League.

Midway through the first half, buoyed by the braveness of this crazy formation by Jim Smith, we broke away and Malcolm Christie scored. Jim had stuck to his plan. We had Kinkladze and Stefano Eranio in the middle and neither of them could be classed as battlers – but they were unbelievable ball players and somehow, that day, they controlled the midfield. They were outstanding.

We got to half-time at 1-0 and, honestly, we were hoping we could hold on for the draw. Manchester City, another team involved in the relegation battle, were playing on the Monday, while Coventry City were playing at the same time as us. They were playing at Aston Villa, who were doing pretty well, so we thought a point at Old Trafford and a Coventry loss would put us in a really strong position on the last day.

As we're walking into the tunnel for the half-time break, the scores are read out:

ASTON VILLA 0, COVENTRY CITY 2.

For fuck's sake. Everyone's expecting United to come out and take us apart in the second half and if that Coventry score stays the same we're as good as relegated. Sure, we're in control of our own destiny, but we're not feeling as positive as we should be. In the dressing room we're all trying to reassure each other, saying that United's attacking philosophy means there will be plenty of chances to counter and get another goal ourselves. Eranio and Kinkladze are pulling the strings and Lee Morris and Malcolm have got plenty of pace as Malcolm has already showed. Coming out for the second half and looking at the quality and energy we had in the vital areas, there was a renewed belief that we might be able to hold on.

The second half was carnage. Bodies everywhere – and however we managed it, we pulled off the win. Steve Round and Jim Smith ran on to the pitch celebrating and my initial thought is that they're buzzing on the back of what is already a momentous result. My response is, "It's great, but we've got Ipswich next week."

"You don't understand," I was told. "Coventry were beaten by Villa – we're safe!" To win at Old Trafford was one thing but to do so and stay up, well, we were having a party on the pitch. We got back to the dressing room and there was a knock on the door. The stewards pushed a massive bin load of beer in – I'm thinking, "Bloody hell, that's good of them!"

It registers about five minutes later – our result, and the Villa win, means that not only are we safe, but Manchester City have been relegated. I don't know if the beer was just a nice gesture of sportsmanship for ourselves or a little bit of fun with City's fate in mind but it made a great occasion for Derby County that little bit better.

We were due to travel to Jersey for a late season training camp prior to our game against Ipswich. To all intents and purposes that was going to be all or nothing, but now, it suddenly meant nothing. We met at Rainsway and a triallist got on the bus, as he was supposed to be coming with us. Next thing, he was asked to leave. "Listen – it's pointless you coming away now," he was told. "This is just going to be a piss-up." The boss didn't come either – I think, after such a long season, he thought that we all deserved to let our hair down and relax.

Steve Round and Sill were taking us, and as much as we knew we could celebrate, we knew Steve would take it seriously too – he is one of the best coaches I've ever worked with. Steve was one of the first to really work in a dedicated way with Prozone and talk to us individually about what was required of us. When I was suffering in the early weeks and months, he stood right behind me motivating me and keeping me on the right path. Steve and Sill were accompanied by Eric Steele – another future United coach – and John McKeown. There was a testimonial game against a Jersey XI – we were told we could do whatever we want, but come Wednesday at 2pm, we were required to be at the hotel ready for the game. We didn't need to be encouraged to go on the piss for a few days – but fair enough, come game time, we were ready.

Now I never thought I'd be writing my autobiography and this lad would get a mention, but there was a complete head-the-ball called Ian Horton who I'd known growing up. I knew he'd moved to the Jersey area at some point but I still wasn't expecting it when there was a knock on the changing room door at the ground and this ginger-haired lad comes through shouting, "Danny, how the fuck are ya!"

He's a massive City fan and I'm sat next to Georgi, so naturally, he's in awe of his former hero. The coaching staff found it hilarious and asked him to do the team talk.

"Awwww, I'm not arsed, just give the ball to Georgi, that's all you do." With that he walked out and left the dressing room.

Sillo and John McKeown actually came on in the game and I think one of them scored a penalty as well – the result barely mattered, it was a charity game for a local cause and I think it served its purpose. At the end of the game, kids came on to the pitch asking for our shirts. Who turns up next to me? Ian Horton. Six and seven-year-old kids want my shirt and Ian barges past them all, "Fuck off you lot, he's my mate." Took my shirt and shorts!

Regardless of that, it was a great trip except that when we got back, loads of us were really struggling – whether it was food poisoning, something we'd picked up or just our body re-adjusting after the alcohol, we were all under the weather. We managed to see the campaign out with a 1-1 draw against Ipswich and I was able to look back on a season where I'd grown in stature and confidence.

It had certainly been a learning curve after all I'd done and been through but with a baby on the way in the summer I was on the path to maturing all round and not just as a footballer. For the first time, I felt fairly confident about saying I was a Premier League footballer – not knowing that a year of change awaited in more ways than one.

08

Down And Out

In the summer of 2001, I was delighted by the birth of my first born son, Jak, to my now ex-partner. Of course, having a child changes everything, it makes you look at life in a different way.

I don't want to be melodramatic but if you take the grim moment where my ban in Antwerp was increased, I could have been finished. Less than two years later, I had played a few games for United but got a move that meant I was on my way to becoming an established player at the top level.

The move from Derby meant I'd finally moved into my own place and now, with a baby boy, for probably the first time I was able to appreciate that there was more to life than football. Before, I would get tunnel vision. I'd get so wrapped up in the game that it was all I would think about. I've now got four kids and aside from the birth of the youngest, who came along when my career was winding down, they were all born at times that gave me a bit of a reality check when I needed it. You realise your priority is your children. Jak came along when we were abroad for pre-season so I flew back early to make sure I was there.

Derby County had a decent pre-season and finished it with a home game against Barcelona – we were 2-0 down in about 15 minutes but I felt I did well in the match. Jim had done away with his 'ducks' formation and shifted back to a 4-4-2, but I'd kept my place on the left side of central defence. I felt like I'd transformed as a player – I'd gained a greater positional awareness and was feeling really good about things.

There was a decent mood around Pride Park as well. They'd tend to try and make a big signing every year and in 2001 Jim had secured the transfer of the Italian legend Fabrizio Ravanelli. Rav had won everything there was to win with Juventus before a famous spell at Middlesbrough. He returned to Italy where he won the Serie A with Lazio in 2000, and it was Lazio he left to join us.

Despite everything he'd accomplished, you couldn't meet a more humble fella – and I hate to throw the clichés in, but he definitely fell into the category of the foreign players who were good for the English game. He was the first out for training and the last in and set a fantastic example for everyone – he also did it on the pitch on his debut too, scoring in a 2-1 win over Blackburn Rovers to give us the perfect start.

Despite the positive mood, there was the cloud of financial difficulty which was starting to hang over many clubs. Derby were no different in this respect and needed to get some money in, so agreed the sale of Rory Delap to Southampton. I was gutted, as Rory was one of my best mates at the club, but I was nowhere near as devastated as the man himself. Rory didn't want to go – he loved the club, loved living in Derby as his wife-to-be was from the town. I remember him coming out of the office when Jim told him. Rory walked around the back of the training ground by himself. No-one ever did that, no-one ever had cause to as there was nothing there, so I followed him. When I found him, he was crying his eyes out. He told me they were selling him – I said he didn't have to go.

"I do, Danny," he said, "The club needs this money to keep afloat. I have to do what's right."

That was Rory all over – selfless to the bone. When players move in situations like that they're often viewed as commodities by clubs, whereas to supporters, it can be portrayed as a player not really caring because they've left for what seems like a decent transfer fee. The situation with Rory really underlined that beyond all of that, players are human and sometimes when they say they don't want to leave, they really mean it. Derby and Southampton were pretty much on a par at the time so it wasn't as if he was making a step up.

Our second game of the season was at Ipswich – where we'd finished our previous campaign – but we couldn't match that result, as we lost 3-1 with Finidi George on fire. In the prior meeting, I'd accidentally injured Marcus Stewart – he hurt his ankle ligaments. This was his comeback game, and I hurt him again – completely by accident again, but I'm sure he was growing sick of the sight of me by that point.

The Blackburn win had proved to be something of a false start as we really began the season poorly. Two scoreless draws followed the Ipswich defeat before four losses on the bounce, the last of which – a defeat at White Hart Lane – was followed by even worse news, when it was revealed that a Leeds United bid for Seth Johnson had been accepted. He went to Elland Road on an unbelievable deal but I was gutted again as that was another great friend gone. Like Rory, Seth wasn't one for 'leaving sinking ships' – when he originally agreed to join Derby from Crewe, he insisted that he see the season out.

Earlier that week, Jim Smith had also left the club – he was sacked and replaced by Colin Todd, and in fairness I think it was Colin's decision to sell Seth to get the money. Colin signed Luciano Zavagno, Pierre Ducrocq and Francois Grenet. Often when a new manager comes in, it galvanises the club but we lost five and won just two heading in to a big pre-Christmas clash with Aston Villa. We battered them and won 3-1.

I'd become quite friendly with Steve Stone after meeting him the previous summer on holiday. Steve was a Villa midfielder and he told me that their manager, John Gregory, had declared that ours was the worst Premier League team he'd ever seen! We beat them comfortably, so he was fuming.

The return fixture was less than a month later and John had been sacked by Villa – they beat us 2-1. As that was Colin's eighth league defeat in three months, he too was sacked – and then John Gregory came to manage us! Colin was great but another example of an assistant not quite making it as a manager – he always took a great interest in me, being a left footed defender, as he was.

Many things can be said about John as he's such a character but I'd go on record as saying he's an unbelievable coach. He came in on his own at first and took all the training sessions.

He ran through really intensive training sessions, saying he was going to test the defenders by overloading attackers until they were completely outnumbered. As an incentive for the attackers, he said that for every goal they scored he would personally do 50 press-ups – and they never did!

We'd suffered another couple of defeats in between Colin leaving and John's appointment and his first official game was against Tottenham at home. Lee Morris scored the only goal in a 1-0 win. We were rejuvenated and won two from our next five games, including a comprehensive 3-0 win against Leicester at Filbert Street.

During that game, Robbie Savage was trying to get all over Georgi as he tended to do. At one point, Georgi did about ten keepy-uppies, Robbie hacked him down, and we got a free-kick. Georgi picked up the ball and handed it to Savage. "Here Robbie," he says. "You can have it now." People always have digs about Robbie – after the game, he and I were selected for the random drugs test, and he was nothing but a gentleman.

Things seemed to be really going well, but then, John made what I felt was a big mistake and relinquished some of the coaching duties to two coaches he'd brought in. I'm not saying they were bad but they weren't quite up to carrying out what John wanted; one of the coaches seemed to have issues with certain senior professionals and that didn't make any sense.

Fab continued to give everything, but even he wasn't immune to the pressure. He was a great motivator for others. Because I was playing well, he was always in my ear, telling me to keep going and that I'd have a good career. You would think with his background and that kind of encouragement he would be able to shrug anything off. Earlier in the campaign, we'd lost 1-0 at Newcastle, and Fab had missed a penalty that would have earned us a draw. The following week we played Liverpool at home, lost 1-0, and he missed another spot-kick. There was a small room next to the dressing rooms at Derby and I found Fab in there after the game, crying and inconsolable. This was Fabrizio Ravanelli, the superstar, feeling like he's a failure.

"What's the matter?"

"I've let the team, everybody, down, we've lost two points now and that's because of me."

"Don't look at it like that – you've been such an influence and role model for me and the younger lads," I tried to reassure him.

He was as passionate as ever in team meetings – after a couple of bad results, he once stood up in front of us and declared, "Listen everybody, we have to have the eye of the tiger. I look around this dressing room and not enough people have the eye of the tiger!"

Despite not having much time in the transfer window, John had managed to bring in Rob Lee and Warren Barton, two hugely experienced players who would hopefully help steady the ship as we battled to beat the drop.

We played Manchester United towards the end of the season at home – Christie scored to give us an early lead, but then they equalised and Juan Sebastian Veron gave them the lead. Then some of the United players started showboating a bit, which is something you don't normally see from them – Roy Keane wasn't playing, and I couldn't help thinking to myself that if he was on the pitch, that wouldn't be happening, and in all likelihood we'd be three or four down.

Throughout this, Warren Barton kept saying, "Keep your concentration lads, we'll get a chance, we will get a chance." He was right – Malcolm grabbed an equaliser, and then put the ball in the net again, only for it to be disallowed when we thought we'd won the game. Literally two days after that, we played at Arsenal and lost 1-0. We gave a really good account ourselves and were really unlucky not to get anything from the game. It was disappointing, but United and Arsenal were the top two teams, so to come away with a point from two games in the space of three days was a bonus.

The real business, we thought, was against Bolton in our next game. We were to travel to the Reebok Stadium knowing a win would put us a point behind them – we were in 19th on 26 points with the three teams above us on 30. With nine games left to play, we felt this one was do or die. Winning wouldn't save us but losing would mean we were as good as down.

We raced into the lead – Christie scored early on, and though Bolton equalised right after half-time, Fab scored his first goal in ten games to give us the lead again. Late on, Lee Morris – fresh, as he's just come on – raced clear of the defence and was brought down by Jussi Jaaskelainen. Penalty. The first one we'd been awarded since Ravanelli missed at Liverpool.

He picked up the ball. Call it a rush of blood, call it what you like, but I approached him and asked him if he wanted to take it – if not, I would take it for him. He looked at me with genuine sincerity. He passed me the ball and said, "Thank you, Danny."

Then it dawned on me – fuck me, I've got to score a penalty now! We were winning 2-1 in the last few minutes and I knew that scoring would probably seal the result. Fortunately I was able to do so, dispatching the ball past Southall (Nicky, not Neville!). I put it right in the side of the net – the keeper's right – and Nicky dived that way. It was like slow motion as it went in, but the celebration afterwards as I ran to rejoice with our travelling supporters was very much real time. Funnily enough, I never hit a penalty to that same side ever again. 3-1, and what a feeling, what a performance.

Myself and Chris Riggott received very favourable write-ups in the newspapers the following day. Though I never allowed myself to go over the top about a result, good or bad, as we travelled home on the team coach, I remarked to Scouse (that was the affectionate nickname we had for John McKeown) and Brian O'Neil that the sunset outside looking amazing. "You've just scored a goal, a penalty, that has secured a massive result and you're talking about a sunset. That just sums you up, dunnit," they said to me.

We'd lost against Sunderland a few weeks prior to the Bolton game with one of the scrappiest goals you'd ever see – and we thought our luck was turning with the win at the Reebok, but in our next game we found ourselves 3-0 down against Everton, who'd just been taken over by David Moyes. We pulled a goal back, Everton scored again, and we managed to stage a fight-back to get it to 3-4 but couldn't quite get a point. It was a case of nearly, but not quite.

We then went on a losing run, suffering defeats in the next four games which put us right in the frame for relegation. It meant a defeat at Anfield would relegate us. We were doomed anyway – it would have taken a miracle even greater than the previous year to get the maximum nine points out of our last three games, but a 2-0 defeat to Liverpool sealed our fate.

As a team, as a club, it was horrible to endure, though there should have been some consolation for me on a personal level as I won the club's Player of the Year awards.

In our last home game, we lost 1-0 at home to Leeds – Robbie Fowler went off injured, and thank heavens he did, because we were so low on confidence that he would have probably had a field day. It was a shame to see everyone so low as we'd been such a close group, particularly before the high profile departures, and we all got on with each other off the pitch as well.

There were a number of factors that contributed to our relegation in 2002 – the instability didn't help and I suppose when you are to look at my comments earlier about average foreign players then you might well say that Derby had their fair share. I don't know if I'd go that far but I'd certainly agree that we had some who might be described as luxuries we couldn't afford. Benito Carbone, who joined on loan from another struggling club, Bradford (who had been relegated the year before), looked really good – a great character again and we got on really well. He left and then went on loan to Middlesbrough and played against us later in the season. If he wasn't contracted to us on a permanent basis, then how were we expected to get the best out of him in that situation anyway?

Georgi, bless him, had all the talent but perhaps not the application he'd shown elsewhere. Though we got on well, we came to blows in one training session when I went in late with a tackle. In fairness, it was pretty bad, but he came up behind me and booted me in the arse. I chased him, he ran away, and Scouse ended up trying to defuse the situation. Kinkladze had all the talent you could wish for but was not suited for this kind of situation. It was talent that would give us an impetus, but particularly in the case of Carbone, he came in, did really well and then left – and we were probably lower in morale than we were when he'd joined! You can't run a club like that.

The summer was obviously a difficult one – I'd left my agent as I didn't think the first one was acting in my best interests. I had to take a loan out to actually pay him off… you live and learn. Fortunately, I was at an age where it didn't really have a long term financial impact on me.

Derby, meanwhile, were obviously counting the cost of relegation and as usually happens, the more sellable assets were linked with moves in the transfer window. I was one, Mart Poom and Chris Riggott were others, Malcolm Christie another – but the club, to its credit, managed to keep hold of most of the squad. If I'd had an agent I think I would probably have left, but I didn't. I thought about the possibility of joining the group that represented Chris Riggott as there was talk of him going to Liverpool – Gerard Houllier was a big fan. Chris thought it was all done and had been led to believe that was the case – when nothing materialised, he was understandably disappointed. Perhaps I was better off.

With the Derby County squad which kicked off the 2002-03 season in the First Division more or less the same as the one that was relegated, there was an obvious commitment for the players to do themselves justice and get back into the Premier League.

That resolve was strengthened when we played a strong Reading team on the first day of the season and absolutely battered them 3-0 – fair play to Ravanelli, he too had stayed, and he was among the goals that day. That evening, we all went out for a meal and the talk amongst us all was how we were going to piss the league.

The next game we had was against the Tony Pulis-managed Gillingham – we lost 1-0 and it was a real wake-up call. It's all well and good playing home games in your Premier League standard stadium but it's the away games that give you a taste of the real life in the division and we were up against it again when we travelled to Grimsby Town four days later.

Without doubt, that game was one of the lowest points of my life. Up front for Grimsby that day was a lad called Steve Livingstone, who had played for Coventry and Blackburn but really made his name at Blundell Park. We both went up for a header and I got there first but ended up heading the back of his head. It really hurt and I suffered concussion. As I'm sat getting treatment I look over and Steve – who is a big, big guy – is motionless on the floor.

Nothing really hit home until I saw the panic on everyone's face and they brought the oxygen on for him. He had blood coming from places there shouldn't be blood and I absolutely shit myself. I honestly thought I'd killed him. It was the worst moment of my career bar none and he left the stadium unconscious.

The game obviously didn't matter to me – at the end I had to go and see the Grimsby doctor, which meant going into their dressing room. Terry Cooke was playing for them on the day and, of course, I knew Terry from our time at United. John McDermott was their captain. I apologised in front of them and said, "That's not me. I would never do anything like that on purpose." I hoped that from the way the challenge was made – going in with my head, honestly, as opposed to my elbow – they

119

could see that the only thing on my mind was winning the ball. Everyone seemed to understand. I called the hospital later to check up on him, I spoke to his wife to apologise and sent her flowers. I was told later on that he had a five or six centimetre fracture in his skull which I'd caused.

I was mortified, as anyone would be, and I accepted responsibility (in as much as I'd caused the event even though there had been no malice) but I was still disappointed to read McDermott angrily describing it as a disgusting challenge a couple of days later in the paper. He was saying I'd done it on purpose – why didn't anyone say that when I went into the dressing room to clear the air? Everyone had seemed okay with me then.

The day after the incident we had an open day at the stadium but I was so ill – possibly with the anxiety, more than likely suffering from the effects of the concussion – that I had to leave.

Though we won that game 2-1, we suffered a really inconsistent run immediately after, losing four from the next five games, leaving us under no illusions about how difficult it was going to be in the lower league.

Things were tougher still for the players as the financial problems which had been exacerbated by the relegation meant there was some speculation about whether or not we'd actually get paid. I spoke with Scott Duxbury again who said that due to a breach in contract, if we didn't get paid, we could negotiate my exit, and I said I wanted to confront the club but not for that reason. Manchester City were interested but all I was bothered about was ensuring that the players received their wages. I thought if I went and handed in my notice, that might force them to pay me – and if they paid me, they'd have to pay everyone. I wasn't interested in leaving.

It was something I thought about for a while with a heavy heart and though I understood the ramifications and what it might mean if the news got out in terms of how my action might be perceived, I decided it was the right thing to do

Brian O'Neil was one of the first to pull me up on it. "What are you doing?" he quizzed. "Do you know how fucking bad this makes you look?" "Bon," I said, "I'm only doing this so the lads will get paid within the next week." "If they don't, you're going to end up looking like a prick and like you're jumping ship," he replied.

I could only hope it would work out – and fortunately, five days later, we all got paid. Fearing the reaction from the supporters, John Gregory said that he would arrange it so that security would escort me into the next game – we were still getting good crowds of well over 20,000. I didn't think we needed it so told him not to bother. As I got to the ground on matchday, there were loads of fans waiting so the security came straight to me. As I walked in, I'm thinking to myself, "Don't react. Be strong. If anyone says anything, just try and explain and leave it at that."

They all started clapping, and then singing my name. "Well done Danny," they said.

Phew – that could easily have gone the other way. Looking back, maybe it was something I shouldn't have done, but I did it for the right reasons.

Things began to get a bit better in the late autumn – we won against both Sheffield clubs but despite a penalty from me in our next game, we lost to a very strong Portsmouth side. Demonstrating how strong the First Division was, our next two wins were against Wimbledon and Watford – two more sides with recent Premier League experience before I scored the only goal in our 1-0 win at home to Brighton. Whatever possessed me, I don't know, but I felt it was right to do a flip to celebrate. I misjudged it and all the weight came down on my right ankle. I tried to hide the limp going back to the halfway line and thought I'd try and get through it. There was a goalmouth scramble and I got involved, thinking it's a perfect opportunity to look like that's where I've picked up the injury and not through my own silliness.

Half-time comes and I approach the manager, "I've gone in there and he's absolutely smashed my ankle." "Yeah, I saw that," he says, and brings me off.

This was mid-December and I'd begun to hear murmurs that there was a possibility that Southampton might come in for me. After a few months in the First Division, with Derby looking as if there was no chance of promotion, I had begun to think that it might be better for me if I was able to get a move in January, back to the Premier League.

I spoke to the physio at half-time and asked if he would take me to the infirmary – in fact, I insisted, and demanded an X-ray once I'd got there. They came back and said everything was fine, aside from a bit of ligament damage but on the Monday morning I went in to see the physio and told him my ankle was knackered. I said that Derby were in a position where they needed to sell players. I was likely to be one so I didn't want it to mess a move up for me.

I missed a few games but returned for the trip to Stoke in mid-January where John made me captain. We won 3-1 and it had become blatantly obvious with the speculation that I was about to leave the club. I was given a great reception by the supporters in the expectation that it was my last game for the club.

I'd got myself an agent in anticipation of a move and as it got down to the last week of the window there was talk that a deal with Southampton was ongoing and being done. The days were ticking on – my agent was saying that Derby were pissing around, but the deadline was on Friday. Monday, Tuesday, Wednesday went without any news. I was in contact with my agent and on Wednesday I said I'd ring Derby. He said, "No no no, don't ring them, I'll deal with it." Nothing happened. I decided then the time was right to ring Lionel Pickering, the Derby owner, God rest his soul – he put everything into the club, it was his life. He'd host a barbecue every summer for the entire team. I felt after everything, it was appropriate if I went to him to get a straight answer.

"Mr Chairman, how are you? It's Danny."

"What are you doing calling me, why are you not in South-ampton?"

"What do you mean – I've been told you're holding up the deal."

"The deal was done two days ago – you should be down there getting your medical done!"

This was Thursday night, at about 9pm. I rang my agent and he said "Yeah, the deal's just been done, you can go down tomorrow." 9am, I went down there, did the medical; the deadline was at 5pm, and at 2pm, I got a contract put in front of me. I said, "Aren't we going to negotiate?" My agent said, "No, we don't have to do that, I've done it, this is your deal."

I opened up the contract – it's less than I'm on at Derby – and I'd taken a 60 per cent pay cut when we'd got relegated!

"What's going on?" I ask him.

"It's just under 22s or 23s, they all get this money, it's either this or stay in the Championship," he responds. With hindsight I should have told him to go and fuck himself. I know now if I'd have told him to stick it and then driven back, I'd have had a phone call while I was on the journey offering me more money.

I didn't – I signed it there and then. I did have a stipulation put in that after 40 games, my contract would be renegotiated – it was only until afterwards I realised how dodgy that deal must have been. Done on a Monday or Tuesday and put in front of me with three hours left?

I have no doubts that it had nothing to do with John Gregory or Gordon Strachan, the Southampton manager, rather the two people who somewhere along the line had become involved in the deal who felt they could get me for next to nothing. There was no chance I'd have signed if that contract was put in front of me on the Tuesday – no chance.

I signed, went back to Derby and then travelled back to Southampton the following day as they were hosting Manchester United. They were now, of course, boosted by the fact that they'd got Ruud van Nistelrooy in their ranks for 18 months. During my last couple of months at United, Ruud had come over to sign for the club and met all the lads, but after everything seemed to be agreed, he broke down in a medical and that put the deal off for a year.

Before the United game, I was stood in the tunnel and Ruud walked past and shook my hand. "Congratulations Danny, this is a great move for you," he says. Bearing in mind he'd only met me once, and then only for two minutes, for him to pay such an interest was unreal. I moved into a hotel room and was followed by my ex-partner who at the time was pregnant with my second child, Jessica, and we got a house sorted fairly quickly.

After relegation from the Premier League, I'd actually felt like I'd established myself as a top level defender and so I was delighted to be back there so quickly – though over the next few months, I would certainly feel out of place as Southampton enjoyed a successful campaign.

09

The Imposter

In the 1990s, Southampton were synonymous with relegation struggles, yet following a move from The Dell to their new St. Mary's Stadium, the Saints were enjoying one of their best campaigns in recent memory under Gordon Strachan. The home defeat to Manchester United I'd observed from the sidelines was one of only two home defeats all season.

Other than eventual champions United, it could be said that Southampton were the team to watch in the 2002/2003 Premier League. Arsenal had won the league and cup double the previous season, so it wasn't really a surprise that they were up competing again as well. Southampton were on course for a great league finish and enjoyed a cup run too – when you looked around that squad, it was no surprise.

Every squad needs a good goalkeeper if they want to challenge and we had two – Antti Niemi first choice with the experienced Paul Jones as back-up. Rory was still there, as well as Claus Lundekvam, while the club had a really strong English contingent with the likes of Wayne Bridge, Jason Dodd, Matty Oakley, James Beattie and Brett Ormerod.

I wasn't at my fittest due to the injury I was still struggling with but I knew my best chance was probably getting in to partner Claus at centre half. My introduction to the team actually came through an injury to Bridge at left back, which meant I was going to make my debut at Ewood Park. Rory's wife was due to give birth – she went into labour on the Friday night, so he had to get a taxi home. From Blackburn! God knows how much that cost him.

The Blackburn game was something of an old boys' reunion – Henning Berg, Andy Cole and Dwight Yorke were in the Rovers team and my direct opponent was Keith Gillespie. Considering it was my first Premier League game for some time I thought I did okay, though we lost the game 1-0. Strachan said I'd be okay once I got a bit fitter.

Gordon is one of those characters in the game that splits opinion but I can honestly say I thought he was an unbelievable manager – he was fantastic at bringing the best out of players. We had a strong squad, but they weren't world beaters and he got them playing to the maximum of their ability. Much of that was to do with fitness, which I'd quickly learned was very important to the manager.

My first training session on the Monday after the United game saw me introduced to a training exercise called 'Poles' and on the first day I couldn't complete it. Yeah, I'd been injured, but there was probably no excuse for me. It was a difficult stamina test for first thing on a Monday morning but after a while we all – me included – began to cruise it. We were so fit and that showed in the results – our stamina levels not only meant we could keep it up for 90 minutes, but we were able to go into overdrive for the last 20 minutes or so which meant we were in a far stronger position to chase or hold on to a result.

There was one game along these lines which immediately jumps to mind and that's a result at the end of the calendar year against Charlton. We were two-nil up, then Scotty Parker scores two unbelievable goals to equalise. You expect then that they'd have the impetus and momentum but we came back and won the game late on. Teams score late goals, sure, but we seemed to be specialists at it. That much was proven a few weeks after I arrived when we got late equalisers in games against Fulham and Aston Villa – Beattie scoring in both of these games to keep him in front of the race for the Golden Boot in a season where both Thierry Henry and van Nistelrooy were scoring for fun.

To have such a group of players playing so incredibly well was a true testament to the ability of the manager, though don't get me wrong, he was still incredibly fiery.

We were playing at Birmingham in April, I was at left back and we conceded a goal just before half-time. Before the game, we'd gone through everything as teams do – who'll be picking up who from corners and setpieces, that kind of thing. The goal we'd let in had been from a corner and there were no on-pitch recriminations but we came into the dressing room and Strachan was going bananas.

"Fucking hell lads, what the fuck is going on?" he yells. No manager likes conceding but Strachan particularly loathes letting in a goal from a set play. "Whose man is it? Whose man is it?" he asks, probably rhetorically. Not for the first time, I open my mouth when it's best not to.

"Gaffer…"

"What Danny?"

"Look at the board – there's a board behind you with the markers on. If you see who's scored then you know who's responsible and we can sort it out."

He went red.

"You what? You fucking what? I tell you what Danny, here's a fucking great idea – next time they get a fucking corner, I'll shout over to the referee and ask him to stop the game a minute so I can bring on the board and we can check who's marking who – you daft little shit!"

He picks up a cup of coffee and hurls it right at me – it misses me and hits our goalkeeping coach.

He'd always seem to catch me at moments that would end up being fairly embarrassing. Gordon wasn't a drinker – though he had every cause to indulge a little as we continued our great season by getting to the FA Cup final. We got beat, narrowly, and another day we might have got a better result against a good Arsenal side. It didn't stop us celebrating – we drank into the night and at the end there was a massive pile-on which I was at the bottom of. The manager strolled past and just said casually, as if nothing was going on, "Night, Danny!"

Getting to the cup final was a fantastic achievement – I'd played against Norwich in the fifth round but that had been my only on-pitch involvement. For the final itself, I was a substitute, and there were a few who had been at the club for a long time who missed out on a spot on the bench. Notably, Francis Benali.

In those circumstances, knowing you'll get a medal come what may, I felt like a bit of an imposter. Particularly with Franny – I felt like I'd taken his place.

The morning after the game I approached him with my medal and asked him to please take it – I said he was a legend and deserved it more than me. On the pitch, anyone will tell you Franny is such a fearsome competitor, he's an animal, but off the pitch he could not be more different. I've never met a more respectful, humble person, and I thought it would be right of me to offer – though, knowing Franny as I did, I was hardly surprised when he declined. I think that the club organised to make sure Franny and a couple of others who missed out did receive medals and rightly so. The club released a DVD about that season and until now that conversation between Franny and I had remained private from my side. It was only on watching that DVD that I saw Franny share the story. I didn't do it for the attention; as far as I was concerned, I felt like I'd just come in and this was the achievement of those who'd been at the club for a lot longer than I had.

We'd proved we could mix it with the best teams and on another day we might have even caused an upset in the final. People had written us off because we'd played Arsenal in one of our last league games and been crucified 6-1. Strachan rested a lot of players that day – I played left back and was up against Jermaine Pennant, who scored a hat-trick. I later linked up with Jermaine when he signed for Stoke and I told him, "I sorted your career out there mate!"

The cup final team was much stronger and the pressure then was on Arsenal – that enabled the lads to give a good account of themselves and the manager made a couple of big calls. First of all he dropped Fabrice Fernandes who had been playing week in, week out, and played a young lad in Chris Baird. Sadly, the extra quality that Arsenal undoubtedly had told on the day – but an extra bonus for us was qualifying for Europe due to Arsenal being in the Champions League.

I suppose 'bonus' is an apt way to describe our last league game of the season, which just so happened to be the last ever league game at Maine Road. Southampton had been around eighth or ninth position all season but three losses out of four games heading into the final game put us in 11th. The bonuses were set up to be dependent on where we finished in the league. I came on as we won 1-0 and it moved us up three places, above City and into eighth.

Considering how I'd started the season, in the First Division and that low point at Grimsby, to now be part of a squad that reached the FA Cup final and finished in the top half of the Premier League was a definite step forward and had at least made me forget about the debacle of the contract situation.

I'd settled in really well – of course, it helped massively that Rory had been there – and felt that when I'd played I had given a good account of myself. With Southampton having done so well, a few of our players were sought after – and naturally, when Wayne Bridge was coveted by Chelsea, I was reassured that competition for that left back spot would be easier, though I have to admit that at this time I was actually favouring playing as a centre half. I thought I was better there than I was at left back and I was at the age where I felt it would probably be best if I had one position and stuck at it – my versatility, and the fact I had a left foot, meant I was something of a jack of all trades and master of none.

It had been quite a transition from playing left wing in my younger days at United to now preferring centre half but I'd really enjoyed it ever since Jim Smith had put me there against Arsenal in a three man defence. With the insurance of having a sweeper behind us, I felt comfortable to bring the ball out. As time went on, that solid introduction to life in central defence gave me the confidence to continue there. I think Gordon liked me more as a centre back too. Still, I would inevitably end up at least playing a few games at left back. At Southampton, we had three other left backs at one stage and I still ended up playing there!

I would have liked to have thought by this time there would be no surprises about strenuous fitness regimes. The first day at Derby was tough and Southampton was tougher still, and considering that was the way they were working midway through the campaign then I guessed pre-season was going to be a nightmare. We went up to St. Andrews in Scotland and I was asking the lads, "What's it like?" "Just make sure you're ready" was pretty much the unanimous response.

After a bit of running down in Southampton we flew up to St. Andrews. It really was a beautiful place, but we didn't stay there. We stayed in what could only really be described as a hostel.

The first thing we did was a six mile cross country run. I'm told by the lads that Paul Telfer will take off like there's no tomorrow and will piss it. Dave Prutton, who signed on the same day as I did, is having his first pre-season at the club too and declares he's going to try and stay with Telfer. "Don't do it Dave, it'll end up in tears," he's warned.

We set off, and as expected, Telfer's shot off. Within a minute we've all been left for dead – all of us except for Dave Prutton. There's murmurs among the lads, "Heck, Prutts can move. He's keeping up with him," they say as we labour behind. Then, Telf is going further and further into the distance and Prutts is coming closer and closer to us.

When we catch up with him he's blowing a gasket – I can't talk, as I'm propping up the back with Rory and Paul Jones – the last thing I am is a long distance runner. Darren Kenton is just about holding his own in front of us but then you hear him yell – his calves have blown up. Man down. We were running in teams and so were getting points for where we finished. Paul Jones ran off and left me and Rory. There was just us two running towards the finish line. I said "What shall we do?" and Rory said something like, "Let's stick together so neither of us finishes last." But honestly, I thought he'd said "No Danny, you just go," so I did – I ran the last 25 yards and beat him by about five yards. We collapsed to the ground, Rory looked at me and said, "You twat!"

There was hardly any ball work; we did have a crossing and finishing routine but even that wasn't enjoyable; we were having to sprint the length or width of the pitch. We started that session with about 30 balls and ended with two or three – whether the lads were hitting them in the bushes deliberately because they were so knackered, I don't know!

Out of a squad of around 25 that travelled only a dozen or so of us ended it fit – Claus Lundekvam's appendix burst, too. We were supposed to go running in the sand dunes but, feeling a little sympathetic, the boss said that if we all went into the North Sea and went out above waist-height then he'd let us off. Most of us did but there were a few who refused because it was so cold. Faced with the prospect of those stragglers being responsible for us having to go in the dunes, we got hold of them and dragged them in.

I was used to the water on that trip – we'd gone down to a harbour one day and Wayne Bridge, who was still with us in early pre-season, jumped in. "Danny," he shouted, "Come in, you won't believe how warm this water is!" I fell for it hook, line and sinker – stripped down, jumped in and I've never been as cold in my entire life. I don't know how he kept a straight face! It was a good bonding trip and despite Wayne leaving shortly after, it was just the kind of trip the club needed to continue to benefit from the optimism that had surrounded Southampton at the end of the '02/03 season.

It worked, too – we were unbeaten in our first six games, getting a good draw at Elland Road, a last minute winner against Man Utd, and a comprehensive win at White Hart Lane. There was that great game I mentioned earlier against Charlton and then the following week we won at Anfield. That win took us above Liverpool and into sixth place in the table.

Our league form softened the blow of our UEFA Cup exit, which is another story with a strange Strachan anecdote. We played Steaua Bucharest and drew the first leg 1-1 at home in a game I didn't play in. My daughter, Jessica, was born on October 12th, just before the return leg in Romania on the 15th.

We knew a hostile atmosphere awaited us but a large number of Southampton fans had travelled. We put on a great performance and with about 10 minutes to go it was still goalless despite us having great opportunities through Telfer and Beatts.

On another day, we'd have scored, but against the run of play, they score a late goal. We go out 2-1 on aggregate but Strachan appears quite happy with us afterwards. "Lads, I cannot fault you, we've gone out, but how we've not won that game is beyond me... that's football. One thing I do want to ask, though – why did you go for it when it was late on and goalless, we had another half hour of extra time!" he says.

He's looking at all of our faces. "By the looks of it, you didn't know?" Then he goes into a rage. "You fucking idiots!"

I'm first in the firing line.

"Danny, what did you think?"

"Gaffer, being completely honest, I was sure that 0-0 meant we were out on away goals."

"You're a fucking idiot!" He goes around all the players, they all say the same thing, he's calling them all the names under the sun until the last player, Jo Tessem, insists that he thought it would have gone to extra time. I didn't know if he was taking the piss to avoid a bollocking. But at that point I wasn't even sure what was real anymore. The fleeting thought crossed my mind, 'well if you knew, why didn't you tell us?!'

"Lads," Strachan finishes. "I'm so proud of you but you have let yourselves down, and do yourselves a favour, if any of youse ever write an autobiography, do not put this is in it. You will look like the biggest bunch of pricks ever." With that, he stormed out of the room, and smashed his foot into a metal skip. How he didn't break his foot, I don't know.

The lads go in the shower and we're in disbelief. Aside from the devastation of going out anyway, we're now starting to feel like we'd let ourselves down when we had previously felt proud of putting a shift in. As a full back, I'd really bombed forward in that last 20 minutes trying to help us get a goal. Jo was insisting that he knew.

Next thing, Strachan pops his head around the showers. "Lads, looks like I'm the fucking wanker here. Youse lot were right and I was wrong. Have a good shower!" Typical Strachan but at least it gave a lighthearted and humorous note to take the defeat on the chin.

The Anfield league win meant that our next game, against Portsmouth, could potentially see us in the top four. Portsmouth and Southampton have one of the oldest rivalries in football and though we'd literally just played them in the League Cup – and won 2-0 – this was the first time the teams had ever met in the Premier League.

The atmosphere was unbelievable – full credit to the Portsmouth fans who travelled in their numbers and made a lot of noise. The cup result had been great and we took that into the league game. Jason Dodd, the long-serving Saints defender, gave us the lead when his corner went straight in. We won the game 3-0 with a couple of late goals to seal the result; it sent the fans home happy as we'd gone fourth heading into Christmas and their closest rivals were in the relegation zone.

By the time it came to the return game, it was a different story altogether – Portsmouth are a very difficult team to go to and a lot of that is to do with their uncompromising home ground of Fratton Park. Travelling there, we had armoured guards escorting us. Portsmouth fans are very passionate and outside the ground they had a big sign saying 'WELCOME TO HELL, SCUMMERS.' 'Scummers' is what Portsmouth fans would call Southampton, while 'Skates' was the nickname they got in return.

We lost that game 1-0, which was tough but nowhere like the humiliation we'd suffer down there a year later. It was a different team in 2005 to the one which started the 2003/04 season. It's amazing how quickly things can change.

10

Blurred Lines

We didn't have the best of times over the Christmas of 2003. Three defeats in four league games and a third round exit in the FA Cup had seen us slide down to ninth in the league and suddenly saw the manager under a bit of pressure.

A win over Leeds earned a stay of execution but then we went to Old Trafford. Louis Saha scored on his debut and United went 2-0 up. We battled back and drew level, but then they scored what turned out to be a fortunate winner through Ruud van Nistelrooy. He was very good at starting offside and getting back level but on this occasion he'd not quite got back onside, which obviously meant the manager was fuming.

We could fill another book talking about my bad boy of an overhead kick which almost made it 3-3 and rescued us a point!

Roy Keane was marking me at corners, I ran to the near post but the ball went over both our heads. One of our lads headed it back and I've somehow thrown myself into an overhead kick from ten yards out. Tim Howard got a touch to divert it on to the crossbar – it hit the bar twice and was near enough on the line, but Paul Scholes got in to clear it.

A draw against Fulham didn't raise any hopes ahead of a trip to Arsenal, who were in the middle of what would turn out to be a season-lasting unbeaten run. During the game, Ray Parlour elbowed me full in the face. They played on – despite it clearly being a free-kick – and scored in that phase of play to seal the result. Ray came up afterwards and apologised but it was a farce. We should have got something from that game.

I felt that was a problem creeping in at the time where too many referees felt they wanted to be pally with some of the top stars and better teams. It did feel sometimes as if they would look down their noses at some of the so-called 'lesser teams'. Supporters don't come to see the referee, they come to watch the game between two football teams, but too many referees want to be the centre of attention. The best referees are the ones you don't notice.

When I was at Derby, I remember a referee's decision that worked in our favour. We were playing Coventry at the old Highfield Road. Mustapha Hadji, clear as day, spat at me. I'd gone through on a tackle and even though I'd heard the whistle, I didn't pull out – it was one of those just to let him know I was there. He spat at me as a result – I went bananas. The referee hadn't seen it, but the linesman had. Hadji got sent off, and next thing, I've got big John Hartson coming over to me. John's a fearsome character and approaches me aggressively.

"What the fuck you doing?" he shouts, "You've just got him sent off there!" I explain that he spat at me and John's demeanour changed immediately. "Fair play," he says. "That's fucking disgusting." That was the kind of character that you would come up against – hard as nails and as intimidating as anything but, crucially, honest. They knew what was fair on the pitch.

There were many tough characters in the game. Graeme Souness was another. I got an insight into how fiery he could be at St. Mary's in October of 2003 when we came up against Blackburn Rovers.

It was a bit of an intense game and there was some needle between Souness and Dennis Rofe, who was one of our coaches. When Souness had been manager of Southampton, Dennis had still been at the club, and they were at each other on the touchline about some of the refereeing decisions.

As we're coming back in from the game, Souness is shouting, "Come on Rofey, let's have it now, you and me. Let's find a gym and get it on." He's taking off his tie and passing it to Tugay, their midfielder, and then starts unbuttoning his shirt.

Holy shit – I'd heard a lot about Graeme's reputation as a no-nonsense character so I'm obviously a bit concerned for Dennis. Of course, Gordon knows Graeme as well as anyone in the game so he tries to act as peacemaker.

"Graeme, come on, calm it down, leave it," he protests. Souness picks Strachan up under both arms and moves him to one side – it just looks hilarious.

"Alright," drawls Strachan, almost dismissively. Thankfully Dennis had retreated to the sanctuary of the dressing room away from danger. Fair enough – Graeme was definitely ready to rumble.

I don't know the politics of what happened at the club but Gordon, being how he was, was seen as abrasive to some. There was speculation that he'd decided not to stay on beyond the end of the season and because that had been leaked, he was effectively forced to resign. Steve Wigley was named caretaker manager and oversaw the next two games, both of which were draws – the first against Everton, which saw a young Wayne Rooney score twice. Steve was a great coach but in my opinion never a manager. I'll get on to the deeper problems later on but for this spell, he was never considered as a serious successor to Strachan.

Rupert Lowe, the chairman, spoke to a few of the senior players to let us know that Glenn Hoddle was coming back. He'd left under a bit of a cloud and a large percentage of the supporters still hadn't forgiven him for jumping ship to Spurs and then signing Dean Richards (God rest his soul) who was an absolutely outstanding defender. That double whammy hurt a lot of fans and they weren't overwhelmed with the prospect of him coming back.

Rupert sounded out the players and said there would be a press conference to appease the supporters. I'd never worked with Glenn but I'd heard unbelievable things about his style and the way he coached. The only criticism I'd heard was that because he was that good a player, he would sometimes get frustrated that others weren't as good – I later learned that Roy Keane was just like that, too. It might be generous to say that the reception to Glenn returning was lukewarm among fans as speculation grew but the players were buzzing about it.

Then, all of a sudden, Paul Sturrock was announced as the new manager, completely out of the blue. The truth, in my opinion, was that Rupert bottled it – he was too scared of the backlash. Yeah, there might have been some grumbling, but once he'd racked up a few points, the fans would have been alright. It's just my opinion but it was a bad call.

With due credit to Paul, though, we weren't to know that immediately as he got a few good results, beating Liverpool in his first game, to mention just one. A 1-0 defeat at Fratton Park followed that but then we won against Spurs and hammered Wolves away 4-1. That was a great game – Claus had never scored for the club, but I sometimes wondered how that was the case. He got in to some amazing positions and always had opportunities but I guess it was a case of, 'right place, wrong person!' He scored against Wolves and he didn't know what the hell to do – we all piled on top of him.

A couple of weeks later we got another good away win, 3-1 at Manchester City in their new home. That result had us in ninth – a respectable position – but losing three and winning none of our last five matches saw us drop to 12th. A clear regression from the previous year with the only bragging rights being the fact that we finished two points above Portsmouth (which probably says all you need to know about the post-Christmas turmoil at the club, considering our respective positions after the 3-0 win in December).

I felt sorry for Paul – I just think he couldn't quite handle the pressure, and he was thrust into the spotlight quite suddenly. That feeling was probably shared by a few of the people behind the scenes at the club who had begun to realise, by the time that the pre-season for the next campaign had started, that he probably wasn't the right man. Instead of dealing with that honestly, I was disappointed that it was portrayed as some of the players turning against Paul. We went away to Austria and there was something on the back of one of the papers saying the players called Paul 'Worzel Gummidge' and he'd lost our respect. Absolute bullshit – that had been planted, probably by someone at the club who wasn't a player, to try and turn things against him. None of the players disliked him and that leak did not come from any of us. They just wanted rid of him.

We put the turmoil of the pre-season behind us and despite losing our first game of the season away to Aston Villa, we beat Blackburn 3-2 in the second game. The day after the game, the lads were called in for a meeting at the club. We're feeling positive about the start we've made to the season, so despite mounting speculation, we're not necessarily expecting any major news. In fact, I say to one of the lads jokingly, "Imagine if they're telling us the manager is leaving." It's merely a joke – Paul's literally just moved into his new house, after all.

Then he stands in front of us all in the canteen and he's shaking – near enough in tears. He says, "Listen, lads... I've been told I've been relieved of my duties." We were all shocked, and felt that it had all been handled very disrespectfully.

Yes, I thought the move up was probably a step too far for him, but that's not necessarily his fault. A few of us really did feel for him and we had given him our full backing – it'd been made to look as if we'd shit all over him. It was a panic appointment at the last minute and their next wasn't any better, when they decided to appoint Steve Wigley on a permanent basis.

It's a very dangerous line to cross from assistant manager or coach to manager, particularly at the club you're already at. As a coach or assistant you're there to laugh and joke with the players, earn their trust and be the go-between, whereas the manager needs to have that distance, and Steve wasn't able to do that.

He suffered a terrible start. After a run without a win, we travelled to Everton. Steve was giving a few younger players the opportunity and that was fair enough, nobody had a divine right to be in the team. I was one of those not seeing much action. Before the game at Goodison Park, Claus Lundekvam was clearly not well, spewing up, and Steve came up to me and said, "If Claus isn't right, you'll be playing." "Cheers," I replied, appreciating the heads-up. Ten minutes later, Claus was ruled out and the team-sheet was named – I'm not on it, Darren Kenton is. I wouldn't have had a problem if he'd been straight, but even though I was pissed off, I thought it wasn't the best time for me to take it up with him. We lost 1-0 and I went in to see him on the Monday.

"What you've done there is out of order, it's disrespectful. You've told me I'm playing and then you've put Darren in – I've no issues with you putting him in but you should have told me you'd changed your mind."

He went off his head – we nearly came to blows. He had a tactics board where all the players were listed according to the team we were in – first team, reserves, youth players. He picked mine off and said, "Fuck you then, you can go and train with the reserves. This is you, right over there." After that, he didn't speak to me, and didn't pick me. I was on the bench for a game against Birmingham and then didn't get a single minute in the League Cup against Colchester – who were unlucky not to get a result.

Next game, we play at Arsenal and I'm in the team. I'm buzzing – we get a very good 2-2 result, I feel like I do myself justice and I'm pleased for Rory as he gets two goals. We're probably unfortunate not to win as we took the lead with five minutes left and van Persie equalised in injury time. In training the following week, Steve brings out the Prozone stats for the recent games and shows them to the lads.

"Look at your average positions for the Colchester game," he says. No disrespect to the other lads but it's like Rag-Arse Rovers, they're all over the place. He shows us the information for the Arsenal game and we've all done really well. We all get praise, me included.

Next game, we play West Brom, and he's fucking dropped me again. I say to him later on, "Listen, you said all this stuff about Prozone, Colchester, and how well we've done against Arsenal. What does that tell me? Even if I play well, I'm going to be dropped."

"It was your fault for the second goal," he responded.

I didn't think it was good enough, even if he was right about that. Look, I've no odds with him as a coach. He's excellent and has proven that since by working with England and Manchester City but I just don't think he had the right kind of attitude, or approach, to be a manager.

I think if you were to ask him he would admit that it wasn't right for him. There were blurred lines – yes, he had proved he could be authoritative by saying I had made a mistake but he hadn't been straight with me over the Everton episode, and it becomes difficult ground to walk on when you've been a coach of a player and are trying to get their respect as a manager.

After one loss he came into the dressing room and went ballistic and then walked out. We were all taken aback but a few of the lads said, "You know what, we deserved that, and we probably needed that. It's probably about time as we're not performing well." Two minutes later he came back in and apologised. You can't do that – and I think that in a nutshell sums up why he didn't succeed.

His last game was a 3-0 defeat to Man Utd at Old Trafford, which is no disgrace in itself. I played and thought I did okay against Cristiano Ronaldo – Steve came up to me afterwards and said, "Thank you. Whatever happens with my job, at least I know you were always behind me."

Of course I was, that was never in question – but I have an opinion and that was that he just wasn't a manager. I would go as far to say that he's one of the best coaches I worked under. The sessions he put on were fantastic and he was one of the main reasons the club was producing good young players.

Like Paul Sturrock, but for different reasons, it was just a step too far.

11

Saints & Sinners

For arguably the first time since the creation of the Premier League, this was an era when there were huge changes taking place in the game itself. In 2003, Chelsea had been taken over by Roman Abramovich and in the summer of 2004, the Russian brought in Jose Mourinho to try and elevate his new club above the 'Invincibles' at Arsenal.

The best thing for a club like Southampton at a time when everything was changing so massively was stability. We didn't have that. I'll always say that if a struggling team makes more than one managerial change throughout a season then you might as well expect the worst.

In 2004-2005, when there was clearly a lot of money to be spent in the transfer market, perhaps one of the best qualities for a manager to have had was an ability to pull off a good transfer. With the winter transfer window looming, maybe that's what made Harry Redknapp seem like the ideal successor to Steve Wigley.

I've spoken to numerous people over the years about Harry, about their opinion of him, and our differing experiences. Nobody ever has a bad word to say about him. My own personal opinion of him from our time at Southampton was that he didn't really want to be there. That was the strong impression I got. He'd taken a big risk coming to the club as a Portsmouth legend and it's just my recollection that he never seemed happy at St. Mary's. This isn't a reflection of Harry's capabilities – from everything I hear, he's still an exceptional man manager now and I will be the first to say that I felt he should have got the England job. In my view, he didn't miss out on the job for football reasons – I thought he was the outstanding candidate in that sense.

In fairness to Harry, perhaps part of the reason he didn't seem thrilled to be at Southampton was because it wasn't exactly the happiest place to be at that time. He tried his best to pull off some signings in January but I wasn't convinced that some of the lads who came in were dedicated to the cause of helping us escape relegation. It is difficult for those who come on loan because the club isn't their be all and end all – what happens to the club doesn't really affect them.

In March, 2005, we played against Man Utd in the sixth round of the FA Cup and got battered 4-0 – it was an absolute embarrassment. For those of us who'd been there for a couple of years or longer, it was obviously a huge disappointment to reflect where we'd come from and where we currently were.

In the dressing room, I didn't hold back.

"It's a fucking disgrace. Some of you lads don't look like you give a fuck."

"Go on then Danny, name names," says the manager. "Say who it is."

Perhaps not the wisest move, but that's exactly what I did.

"You've got two talented players here, two very talented players, Olivier Bernard and Henri Camara, but out there today they didn't look like they were bothered."

"Oh you can't do that, you can't name names!" Harry says.

I've no problem admitting that Camara had and has far more ability than me – I worked with him again at Stoke. Same goes for Bernard, he had great ability. That's not what I was questioning. You can't just turn up when you feel like it. What frustrated me more than anything was that I knew what they were capable of. You can't carry passengers in a relegation fight and I'd learned that already with Derby. Added to that, someone like me couldn't afford not to give a toss; I had to give everything every single game just to keep my place.

I'm not saying that Henri and Olivier were the reasons or even the catalysts – the club had suffered from so much mismanagement prior to their arrival that relegation almost felt like it was inevitable, no matter how hard we tried. This is with the benefit of hindsight, of course.

There were a couple of stages under Harry where we pulled off very good results and had a brief feeling that we might pull off an escape. We defeated Liverpool 2-0 and then had a run of five games without losing – two wins on the bounce against Tottenham and then Middlesbrough when Peter Crouch was unplayable.

The five games that followed saw us lose four times with the last of those defeats being the abysmal capitulation against Portsmouth. We lost 4-1 and that meant we were bottom – they'd all but guaranteed their own safety with the win, and as you might imagine, their supporters' delight was intensified by the fact they'd achieved it over Harry. That wasn't the last say that our local rivals would have in our fortunes that season.

Our final three games were against Norwich City, Crystal Palace, and Manchester United – the first two, games against fellow strugglers with no relegation place yet guaranteed, and though the final game was against United, they were in the FA Cup final and it was anticipated they might well rest a few players.

Camara, to his credit, got that run off to a flyer – a dramatic late goal against Norwich decided a 4-3 scoreline in our favour (the less said about my own goal the better) and going into the penultimate game at Selhurst Park, we were above Palace on goal difference. The game was high pressure and we knew that defeat for either team was good as certain relegation. Palace took the lead but Crouchy scored a penalty a few minutes later. Then, in the second half, Crouchy was sent off. I turned to Andy Johnson, the Palace forward, and said, "That's us fucked."

He'd been massive for us. Harry certainly got the best out of him and transformed him from a player who everyone knew had the potential to a player who showed it. Crouchy was the one who made a difference; he was the one who would give us a chance.

Our heads were down and the former Inter forward Nicola Ventola scored for Palace – 2-1 going into injury time. Then I scored in the last minute to give us a chance going into that final week. It was a chance, and that was all we could ask for. We were in 18th, but with a favourable goal difference over Norwich, who were a point above us in the last safe spot of 17th. Norwich hadn't one away win to their name all season and were at Fulham on the final day – a draw might be enough for us.

Despite United's impending Wembley date, there could be no suggestions that Sir Alex fielded a weakened side at St. Mary's – Ferdinand, Giggs, Rooney, and van Nistelrooy all started. Against the odds, we took the lead through a John O'Shea own goal and actually looked in control until Darren Fletcher equalised. United turned it around and their pressure told when van Nistelrooy scored the winner. Despite our efforts to get a point, we lost the game and ended up bottom.

The team who were bottom going into the last day, West Brom, had beaten Portsmouth with a late winner to guarantee their safety. Palace also went down and Norwich not only lost as expected but got annihilated.

It was one of the most unpredictable final days in Premier League history – at some point throughout the afternoon, all of the teams involved in the relegation fight were safe.

As a player, you hear things from the fans but it's more through the general atmosphere, whether they're cheering or whether they're silent or anxious that lets you know how things stand elsewhere. For us, we were in control of our own destiny, so we knew that a win meant it wouldn't matter what happened elsewhere.

It was my second time being relegated and I can't describe how low you feel in the immediate aftermath. It was the first time Southampton had been relegated from the Premier League.

I've already spoken about the various pressures that are associated with going down and how that extended far beyond the playing staff.

After the game I was dejectedly walking towards the dressing room; I was just about the last player making my way back there. Waiting for me outside was Sir Alex. He stuck his hand out and offered it to me, saying, "Danny, I know it's a horrible situation and I'm sorry for that. I had to play this team today – there was nothing I could do." Once again, it was something that he didn't have to do, these were things he had to say. It was the act of a man with immense integrity and empathy and I was grateful for his comfort – though, in the cold light of day, it was small consolation.

It's always difficult for a player in those kind of situations to assess how they did. I felt I'd got better as the season wore on – it wasn't my greatest year, but I did okay, yet obviously I'd been part of a team that had been relegated, so how well did I really do? People might look at my comments about the number of managers that we had and say they're excuses – I don't care if we had six managers, that doesn't change my performance and my opinion of it. I'd been in my favoured position of centre back and, like it or not, was part of the team that had seen this great club relegated.

I've mentioned a few players, but I did want to reserve special mention for Jamie Redknapp. Jamie was struggling really badly at the time with injuries but was brought in by his dad to do a job. He would have ice around his knees for the entire time after games and could barely walk properly, but he gave every last ounce of himself for the club despite the troubles we were in. He gave everything on the pitch and I have nothing but the utmost respect for his contribution. He conducted himself impeccably, was a fantastic example around the club and did not deserve his final game to be one that he suffered relegation in. Sadly, that was the case, and there was intense speculation during that summer that there would be more change at the top.

I was glad that Harry didn't leave in that summer of 2005. I was hoping that he would rekindle some of the magic in the second tier and do what he did with Portsmouth in taking us up. To all intents and purposes, by the time he had taken over at Southampton we were a ship already sunk or destined to be so.

In the pre-season of the '05/06 campaign he brought in Dave Bassett and also Dennis Wise, two individuals experienced at the tougher end of the footballing spectrum. He also strengthened the squad with a few Polish lads and Darren Powell from Crystal Palace. We started the season fairly well, drawing our opener against Wolves and losing against Luton, though we won our next three games. We then drew our next five, a run in which I scored at home to QPR, before we came up against Reading. They were by far the strongest team in the division but we absolutely battered them. We drew 0-0, but if we'd have beaten them 7-0, they wouldn't have been able to complain. Dave Kitson was on their side that day and it's a game we still talk about to this day. They went from strength to strength but the same couldn't be said for us.

There was a consistency in results – the run of league draws extended to eight consecutively in total – but despite the introduction of Theo Walcott who had come through the ranks and made an instant impression, scoring in a couple of 2-0 wins for us over Millwall and Stoke, Rupert Lowe still seemed intent on having his say. Following relegation, Rupert had made the controversial decision to appoint rugby coaching legend Sir Clive Woodward as a 'performance director'.

In sport, it's often suggested that one sport can learn from the techniques and methods of another, and with Sir Clive achieving the ultimate success in the game with England in the Rugby World Cup of 2003, it had been mentioned quite often in the media that he might be the man to bring a revolution to the round ball game. His appointment at Southampton was probably more likely down to his friendship with Rupert and was still seen as radical when it was made. I've all the respect in the world for Sir Clive and what he did in rugby but problems became instantly apparent when he seemed clueless of the actual rules of the game. One day, he asked one of the masseurs what 'offside' was.

Behind the training ground we had an indoor astro turf pitch; a ridiculous amount of money was spent on technology in this centre for pointless things like eye tests on computer systems. This was money that was far better being invested into the team. Although Harry continued to put on a public front that everything was okay, you could clearly understand and share his frustration.

Things came to a head after a home game against Leeds – we went 3-0 up at half-time and ended up losing. We went in the day after the game as Harry called a meeting. Sir Clive was there, Dave Bassett, Kevin Bond, and Harry, all sat on the top table. The meeting started about the game but then seemed to go off on a tangent. Midway through, Harry turns to Dennis Wise.

"Can I ask you something, Wisey?"

"Yeah, sure boss."

"Rupert Lowe says you've been going to him to talk about things at the club. That's fucking out of order. We don't let anything go out of the dressing room, you know that."

Dennis tries to explain himself.

"Boss, he asked me a few things on the football side, so I just gave him my opinion."

"It's fucking out of order. That's not how we do things."

Wisey goes quiet for a bit – in the few months he'd been at the club, I'd got to know him quite well and I'm thinking, 'Bloody hell, that's not like him'.

Next thing, Wisey stands up.

"Harry."

"Yeah?"

"We're putting all of our cards on the table, are we?"

"Certainly."

"Okay. Well why don't you tell that fella sat beside you what you really think of him."

He means Clive, of course… Holy shit, talk about opening up a can of worms. That was Wisey all over.

They both had a point, though, and from Harry's point of view, if he wasn't able to continue with full control as a manager should, then it seemed a matter of if, not when, he was going to leave.

After less than a year in charge, it was announced that Harry had walked out – his initial departure from Fratton Park had supposedly been due to problems with not being allowed to do the job by himself and it was no surprise that when push came to shove this time around, Harry wanted no more of it.

He returned to Portsmouth and went on to pull off the 'great escape' in their own relegation battle of 2006. That was great for him and fair enough – I think he was far happier there. There's nothing wrong with that. He had an affinity with the club and the fans that he never really managed to establish at Southampton and for a period of time there was a power shift on the south coast. They were the top team in the Hampshire area.

A couple of weeks after Harry left we had a game at Norwich and lost – Sir Clive came in afterwards and started comparing throw-ins to line-outs. He was bringing rugby analysis to football and it was farcical. I'll give credit where it's due and say Sir Clive was fantastic with some of the younger players but it felt like the first team was being neglected in preference for new methods that didn't seem to have any place in football. Of course, Sir Clive's methods were backed fully by Rupert but it goes without saying to almost anyone who reads this that it just seems utterly illogical to have a man in charge of analysing performance when he openly admits to not having a strong grasp of the basic rules of the game.

I had approached life in the Championship in much the same way as I had done when I'd first suffered relegation with Derby. I was dedicated to helping the Saints get promotion and was trying my hardest to do so, yet that wasn't helped by contract problems I'd been having for quite some time. After the nonsense surrounding the contract I'd signed when I joined in the first place, I'd at least been satisfied that it would be reviewed, as agreed, when I'd played 40 times for the club.

There'd been no mention of this despite the fact I'd passed that milestone at the end of the 2003/4 season. I'd taken around a 40 per cent pay cut when we got relegated, which was fair enough. That was in my contract after all. What I couldn't understand was why the club were happy to acknowledge the clauses in my contract when it came to taking money off me but not the other way around. Over time, in that season in the Championship, I'd begun to get very bitter about it, and when we saw money being spent on what we felt were ridiculous things, a few of the players began to resent the situation. We would have been appeased had Harry not had his hands tied; if he'd been able to get in one or two of the players he really felt would get us back up. Regardless of that, and our bad run of results which followed Harry's departure, it wasn't in my mind to angle for a move.

George Burley came in to replace Harry and one of my first dealings with him was to discuss my situation. Birmingham came in for me on the last day of the transfer window – at the time, they were in the Premier League. Another player might have pushed for a move. The club rejected the offer and I said it was fine, but that the time was definitely right to discuss my contract.

George accepted that, but as the season wore on, he asked if we could leave it until the end of the campaign. Fair enough, I thought, he had things on his plate with getting used to the club and so on. We enjoyed a decent run of results towards the end of the season but were realistically nowhere near the play-offs. I was also realistically nowhere near a new contract.

We came back for pre-season and I still believed George's reassurances that this new contract would materialise. I got in touch with my agent – thankfully, I'd now got a better agent than the one who had negotiated my transfer to Southampton.

I remember getting rid of that one – he told me in a phone call that he had 'dealt with two players from the Manchester area and you're both massive c**ts'. Nice guy. "Mark my words," he said, "You're only going down after you leave me." The agent I got afterwards became a close friend and looked after my best interests.

Later on, I got a call from my new agent saying I was getting a contract offer coming through. Thank God for that, I thought. Then he called me and said, "Danny, you need to sit down. They've offered you less than what you're on now." Burley said that it was Rupert Lowe's doing.

I consider myself as loyal as anyone, in football and in life, and I can't stand disloyalty in return – I asked George if he would sort it out for me and he said he couldn't as it was the chairman's decision.

At the time, George was bringing in these medical people from Scotland who took a snippet of your hair, tested it, and it told you all the vitamins you needed in order to best look after yourself. George told me I needed to do that and I refused, saying I was going home. My agent called me later to say George now wanted nothing to do with me at the club and I had to train on my own. That was enough for me – I wanted to make sure my side of the story was heard because I knew I was going to be painted in a bad light.

In fact, I knew that was the case already anyway. One night someone threw a brick through my window – thankfully, I was home alone at the time. I was on crutches as I'd done my medial ligament but I went outside with my two labradors and put my car on full beam. I was a sitting duck. It was clearly a disgruntled supporter who wanted to send a message, so I felt it was about time I sent my own. I asked my agent to contact the local paper, I think it was the Southern Daily Echo. I slaughtered the chairman – he obviously had a right to reply – then the club's secretary called me to say the chairman had forbid it from being printed.

"Tell Mr. Lowe it's going in the paper," I replied. I got another call later to tell me that if I didn't pull the article, the contract offer was going to be taken off the table. Unbelievable – I thought it was a wind-up! I said, "You *better* take that off the table, it's a disgrace!"

I got yet another phone call threatening me that not only is the contract offer off the table, but if the piece gets printed, I'll never play for the club again. "Tell him to do one," I responded. The newspaper printed it and a few days later a press officer at the club called me to ask how it felt to be on the transfer list. Nobody had the decency to tell me! I was summoned to go and train by myself and though it went against everything I believed in, I did it.

After learning of my troubles, my old pal John McKeown rung me to say that he'd just moved to Stoke City and Tony Pulis, the manager there, would have me at the club.

He said Tony had big ideas and asked if I'd like him to call me – he did, and I have to say he sold the club to me. It was clear I wasn't wanted at Southampton and this was not a case of me looking to move; Stoke were hardly a club in a far stronger position, it has to be said. It was a move that I felt I had to make.

Approaching my peak years, it was imperative to me to find somewhere where I could enjoy playing football again, though there is no way I could have expected things to turn out the way they did.

12

Battersea Dogs Home

I suppose it could be said by some that money was a factor in my move to Stoke City but the circumstances could hardly be more different. I doubled my wages but that was more of a reflection on how badly Southampton had handled everything with my contract. The move to Stoke certainly wouldn't have been seen as a step up.

For me, the principle of the situation meant I was unhappy at Southampton anyway and was looking for a move. Tony Pulis did such a good job of selling Stoke City to me that even if I'd had been offered the same money I was on, I would still have jumped at the chance because the primary thing for me was finding a place where I could enjoy my football and feel a part of what was happening.

It was Stoke's centenary year and under Tony there were big plans. Based on their historical average position, where they finished in 2005/6 – 13th, beneath Southampton on goal difference – was probably about what they would expect. They had no right to expect promotion but there was an optimism and hope that surrounded the club, though that wasn't initially the case. Tony had rejoined after a year at Plymouth and let's just say he wasn't the overwhelming fans' favourite for the role. They probably didn't want him but Peter Coates, the chairman, did, and he felt Tony was the right man to rebuild the club from the shambles it had become under the prior owners.

I found out very quickly that Stoke fans are among the most passionate and they absolutely love their club. Tony was equally passionate about his visions for the future and that was infectious. When I first met him, he started telling me about the players he was hoping to bring in. There was something reassuring about being trusted in that way. It felt like he really valued my opinion. There was no better example of that than when we were waiting for the contracts to be finalised for my transfer. He asked me in a straightforward manner, "Ricardo Fuller or Dexter Blackstock?"

I said Dexter was a good player but Ricardo had been on loan at Ipswich the previous season and when he came back, he was like a man possessed. Ricardo's ability to provide something off the cuff made him the more attractive buy for Stoke at the time. Tony respected my view and Stoke moved quickly for Fuller.

I felt greater responsibility, too, when Tony shared his concerns about some of the senior players at the club.

There were suggestions that they had too much power and were bullying some of the younger lads who, as a result, weren't coming out of their shell. Tony wanted me to try and bring the group together, and said he intended to bring in more players to try and help that situation while also obviously improving the squad.

All that would happen in time but things didn't exactly go to plan at the start. Our first game of the 2006/07 season was at Southend, where we suffered a disappointing 1-0 defeat. It was a tough time for me personally as while I was away from home, I received a call from my now ex-partner telling me one of our dogs had to be put down. That meant having to break the bad news to my two children over the phone, which was a difficult experience.

That was the night before the game and as I say, the match didn't go well – it was a roasting day and with about half an hour left, Luke Chadwick collapsed from heat exhaustion. I went over to him and he was motionless for a while. They brought oxygen on and it was obviously a pretty scary moment. Thankfully, he was okay. He was kept in a local hospital overnight while we travelled back. We trained on the Monday and to everyone's surprise Chadders was back in training. "The gaffer says that if I play against Derby tomorrow (we had them on the Tuesday) I can take Wednesday and Thursday off," he told us.

It was an early sign that Tony was building a collective team spirit at the club, an attitude that we would work hard for the cause and make what seemed, at times, like personal sacrifices for the club because of the manager. I've now got scars and bumps all over my body where I'd torn muscles and carried on playing. It wasn't bullying, it was a different kind of motivation. Personally speaking, I wanted to do whatever I could for the manager, and perhaps some of that is down to the fact that I was at an age where I was approaching my peak. I'd been through a bit of a bad time but I was desperate to prove my worth. If you looked around the squad that Tony Pulis was trying to assemble then it quickly became apparent that there were a few more like me.

Chadders played against Derby and we won 2-0 – maybe it just wasn't Luke's week as he cracked his head open in that game! At least he had the next two days off, though…

I suffered an injury, too, in that game, when my medial ligament opened up again. I had to come off – I should have been out for about six weeks but I went to see a doctor who was well known in the Leicester area, Roger Oldham. He had some sort of solution which he injected into your joints to solidify them and make them stronger. I think I only missed a couple of games in the end.

My return was in the middle of a run of draws. The results weren't awful but they weren't convincing, it looked like we were just about keeping our head above water. The concerns of supporters intensified when those results were followed by two consecutive defeats – the second of which was at Molineux, where Wolves beat us 2-0.

Clint Hill – who has gone on to have a great career – got sent off for us, which meant that in the following game when he was suspended, a space had opened up at centre half. I'd been playing left back and it's no secret by this point my preferred position was at centre back.

It was a breakthrough for me as I knew I'd get a chance in my favoured role in the next game against Preston. However, the Wolves game had seemingly been a turning point for the supporters who, after nine games, were putting together a petition to call for the manager's head. Thousands of red cards were being distributed with the plan to show them as the manager walked out of the tunnel.

I can't be certain but I'm sure Tony was aware of this and just before the start of the game, he pulled off a masterstroke by signing Lee Hendrie from Aston Villa. That was enough to buy him some time from the fans who were curious to know what the next step was. We drew against Preston – okay, not a great result again, but this was a decent Preston team and we played very well. In the coming days, Rory Delap, Salif Diao and Andy Griffin were brought in and suddenly Tony was forming the base of a team and squad that would be successful. The mood changed instantly and in our next game we beat Leeds 4-0 at Elland Road – that was the start of our ascent. I scored my first goal for the club. We absolutely destroyed them and came off the pitch buzzing.

In our next game, we played Sunderland at home which was Rory's second game for us. Ironically enough, Rory had come from Sunderland on loan and the rule that players couldn't play against their parent club was not invoked for this game; he went into a challenge with Robbie Elliott who was a good friend of his, an innocuous one with no malicious intent, but Rory went down in agony. Rory's a tough lad and I was the first one over to him – I knew it was serious by his reaction.

"My leg Danny, my leg," he screams. I take a look and it's bent, it's all over the place. I try and re-assure him but it was clear to see his shin was in a position it shouldn't have been, it was facing the opposite direction from his ankle. He was taken off and the injury had an affect on the entire team who went flat – Sunderland took the lead and we went into half-time one goal down.

I was concerned and I'll admit straight up that my focus was solely on Rory's condition. He was 30, and the injury was so bad that there was a natural and obvious concern that it might cost him his career. At half-time Tony acknowledged Rory's pain but said we need to use that to our advantage and play the second half for him, win the game for Rory. We were a team transformed and won 2-1 – Rory at the forefront of our minds but as motivation and inspiration rather than distraction. I love Rory like a brother and he'd only been at the club for a few days yet everyone had taken to him. To see not only a fellow professional but also someone I'd known for so long go through that was terrible.

Rory obviously spent some time in hospital and our old friend Scouse went to see him. I called Scouse before I went and asked if Rory needed anything. He said that Rory was still a bit of a mess, hadn't had a shower or anything, so could I get him some boxer shorts. This was about 8pm and everywhere was shut. I didn't know what else to do except get my best, clean pair and take them to him. I stopped at a garage on the way and got some sweets and a massive teddy bear for him to try and lighten the mood. I got to the hospital and gave them to him and then passed him the bag with the boxer shorts in and told him what I'd brought him. Rory just looked at me really strangely – almost ungrateful. I knew Rory, and I knew he wasn't naturally ungrateful, he was very unselfish, so I just put it down to the painkilling medication and tried not to think anything of it.

Tony and John Rudge came in shortly after with Rory's parents so I said my goodbyes and left. Even though he was only on loan at the club, Stoke and Tony really stood by him and wanted him to know that he had their support.

Rory had his operation and was on the mend, and I went around to see Scouse just to have a chat about it. I shared my concerns about Rory being ungrateful and Scouse agreed, he said he thought it was out of order. It wasn't something I was holding against Rory, of course, but it was something on my mind and with Scouse saying I was justified in my concern, it made it more real in a way. A few weeks later Rory was back at the club and I went to see him to make sure he was alright.

"About the boxer shorts…" I started.

"Danny, why the fuck did you bring me boxer shorts?"

"Well, Scouse had seen you and told me that you needed some."

"Danny, I didn't ask for anything."

His wife, Helen, had brought him plenty of clean underwear, as you would expect. Scouse was just winding me up and like a dickhead I fell for it. Stitched me up a treat.

The coming together of the team to get the win in the second half of the Sunderland game was another early indication of the team spirit which would prove so valuable for Tony and the club over the next few years – but there still remained some concern about some of the younger players, who were still needing to come out of their shell. Slowly but surely, the introduction of the new faces meant the phasing out of some of the other senior players and those who remained knew they had to embrace the new era.

It's been said and remarked quite often that the Stoke City side that Tony built in his second stay bore more than just a passing resemblance to the famous (or should that be infamous) Wimbledon side of the late '80s and early '90s. In some respects it's a fair comparison. There were players in that team and squad that many would say were too good for the Championship, players coming towards the peak of their careers that for whatever reason had lost their way in the game. Tony had found a bunch of these players at the right time. While Wimbledon had the 'Crazy Gang' nickname, we had the affectionate moniker of the 'Battersea Dogs Home'.

These players all had to get back on track, and I suppose when you have a number of players with the same individual goal it then becomes a collective one and grows from there. I certainly class myself as one of those players after what had happened at St. Mary's. I remember making that drive up to Stoke from Southampton and when it became public knowledge I was leaving, I was getting phone calls and text messages left, right and centre. "What are you doing?" was the general question, sometimes in less polite terminology. They had a point – it could so easily have been a sideways move and I could have continued to drift. But Tony had sold me the club and I believed in it – it was the fact that others felt the same way that started to eventually move the club forward. It was a gamble, but probably the best I'd ever made.

Stoke weren't a backwards club, they weren't a club who were necessarily struggling with money (more than any other club in a similar situation) but there were certain circumstances which forced us to stick together. The training ground wasn't worthy of the name; it was essentially a pitch and we had to change at the stadium. That meant that some of us would have to drive small groups of lads over to training. There'd be massive arguments beforehand as we knew that meant the cars would get filthy. At most clubs, players do their training and then at 12.30 they're done and dusted, they can leave. We were staying until 2pm or 2.30, until it was time to pick the kids up from school. I'm not saying it was a hard life, the point is that we were spending more time together and it developed a unity which turned into one of, if not our single greatest asset.

We followed the Sunderland win with a loss at Southampton. We battered Norwich 5-0 in a game I scored in, then lost at Leicester before we went on a run which brought a record that still stands today – going seven games without conceding a goal. In that Norwich game, we were battering them 3-0 when we were awarded a penalty. I'd been the penalty taker at South-ampton and I was the closest one to the ball, so I picked it up. Carl Hoefkens, who was a Stoke legend, was the regular taker at the club and was trying to get the ball off me, telling me that he took the pens. I couldn't relinquish the ball as I'd look like a fool but then the supporters in the Boothen End, which is where all the hardcore and passionate Stoke fans are, all started to sing Carl's name. They loved him, idolised him.

But I kept hold of the ball. I just couldn't give it up or I would have looked stupid. Carl went off in a bit of a huff, which I can understand. I put the ball on the spot and the pressure for me to not miss was now far greater than it really should have been with the game more or less won anyway.

Fortunately, I scored. Carl didn't speak to me after the game but later on he did comment on it, saying that he'd taken pressure penalties before and that it was okay for me to do it at

3-0. I could have told him about the instances I'd done it under pressure in the past but didn't want to rock the boat. Tony came out and said he didn't have a problem with what I'd done but I was still interested to see what would happen next time.

I didn't have too long to wait. In the middle of our good run, we played West Brom at home who were doing really well in the league. In the prior game, at Hull, I'd scored in a 2-0 win so was high on confidence anyway, and when we were awarded a penalty with the West Brom game scoreless, Carl came up to me and said I was okay to take the penalty. It was good of him to make that gesture – I was able to at least prove in front of Carl that I could take a spot-kick under some pressure. There was the added drama of Jonathan Greening, who'd obviously played with me at United, going up to Russell Hoult in goal and telling him which way I was going to put the kick. I thought I'd have to be clever with it, so hit it straight down the middle and Russell dived over the top of it.

Overall I scored seven times that season and that was reflective of my form in general. Gradually, the supporters started to get behind Tony's ideas, and we did really well for the rest of the season. Sadly, the run had come at just the wrong time. The difficult start we'd had meant that we were to miss out, just, but still, Tony deserved all of the credit that he got; firstly, for implementing his changes successfully and secondly, for establishing an identity. Reinventing Stoke's image encouraged better quality players like Dominic Matteo and Patrik Berger to join, which gave us an extra boost.

Naturally our great form, particularly in defence, began to attract attention from Premier League clubs and Reading made a January move for Michael Duberry. Michael was our club captain and one of those that were probably too good for the Championship so it was no surprise that Premier League clubs were interested and, with him being 32, it was equally no surprise that he took what turned out to be his last chance to play in the top division.

That meant that as well as freeing up another centre half position, the captaincy was up for grabs. Tony called Darel Russell and I into a meeting to ask which of us wanted it. Darel didn't seem that bothered and said he thought I should have it. It was a really proud moment for me, as though I had been a captain at other clubs, I'd never been the permanent club captain. It goes without saying that this honour was simply cementing the respect I had for Tony and my own good feeling towards the club. I really felt as if I was an integral part of the rebuilding there and to be trusted as the on-pitch leader in what was undoubtedly the best team spirit I'd ever been a part of, was a huge shot in the arm.

The turn in support was illustrated by the attendances for our final two home games of the season as we looked like we might clinch an unlikely play-off spot. 17,000 turned up for the draw against Hull and in our final home game over 20,000 turned up to see us beat Colchester and give ourselves a decent chance of getting into a play-off position on the final day. Prior to the Colchester game, a fantastic year for me was capped off when I managed a clean sweep of the club's Player of the Year awards. I was named as the Club Player, the Supporters' Player and the Players' Player.

There are a small percentage of players who are able to enjoy being part of a team who wins trophies on a regular basis but for the other 99 per cent, happiness and success is relative and mainly depends on three things – how often you're playing; how well you're playing, and how welcome you feel at the club. All of those three boxes were ticked for me at Stoke and I'd never been happier.

That said, there was still disappointment around the corner. We could only draw at QPR on the last day and that meant we didn't make the play-offs. I was devastated as I'm certain that if we had, we'd have got promoted. I don't say that lightly – aside from the two teams who had been promoted automatically, we were the best team in the league, there was no question about that in my mind. It's not just talk, I think it's backed up by what happened next. Derby were the promoted team through the play-offs and went on to be the 'worst team' in the Premier League era. Stoke would go up a year later and Tony's record there speaks for itself.

We were good enough to beat any team in the league and give them a proper going over too, no problem, but we simply started our run too late. We were brilliant at hitting goals in quick succession to punish teams – there was a game at West Brom in the run-in where we went 3-0 up in 22 minutes. We weren't just sitting on results, we were proving how good we were. Leeds, West Brom, Cardiff – all beaten by comprehensive scorelines. The team had developed and gained in so much confidence and self-belief that there was genuine astonishment that we failed to get the result at QPR. I had a goal disallowed on the day but I'm not sure that even if we'd have won, results were going our way.

To further illustrate the point about our quality, we battered Derby home and away. The away game, though it should have been a real high, turned out to be one of the low points in probably my entire career. We did well and I scored a penalty in a 2-0 win. I've never held any grudges and I certainly hadn't left Derby on bad terms. I thought I'd had a good relationship with the fans there – but at the end of the game, I walked over and applauded the away fans, then made my way towards the tunnel. As I got there, one of the Derby supporters was going on at me.

"Higginbotham, you're fucking shit, you're a wanker!" he was yelling. He wasn't the first to give me grief, not the last, so I just tried to block it out and kept walking. He carried on, I turned to have a quick look at him and I saw that the bloke giving me all this grief had got his four or five-year-old son with him! I shouldn't have done what I did, but that really made me angry, so I approached the fella and called him a clown, told him he shouldn't be swearing in front of his kid.

That didn't stop him, just revved him up to hurl more foul-mouthed abuse. A few more Derby fans saw this and came towards us. Thank God, I thought, they'll make him see sense – but they joined in with him! I saw red and I started to move forward and go for him – I knew it was the wrong thing but I just couldn't stop myself. Thankfully, a few of the players had noticed and grabbed me and pulled me back. Once in the dressing room I was able to calm down but I was still a little annoyed by this shithouse who was doing that in front of his kid. Look, I'm no angel, you've read enough to know I'm no stranger to bad language, but there's a time and a place. What example was he setting to his kid?

To be fair – what example did I nearly set? Thankfully the lads were looking out for me and helped me out on that occasion. What might have happened if they hadn't, what action might have been taken? I wasn't a hothead, I'm not that way. If anything, I see myself as the peacemaker, the voice of ration and reason. Confrontation isn't for me. I wasn't a particularly dirty player – I was never sent off and I don't think I ever picked up a suspension through accumulated bookings.

Yet I'd been so close to major incidents. It was proven in Belgium that I was the victim of lies, but that doesn't stop the fact that what happened, happened... as much as I'd like to say the incident at Derby was all the fault of someone else, I can hold my hands up and say I crossed the line, there's no doubt about that.

The next day, the local paper covered the incident and printed a picture of me looking really angry – that paper went straight in the bin. I didn't need my six-year-old boy seeing that. It just goes to show that sometimes, logic can play no part. How could it have? This was just an isolated incident and you get idiots anywhere, but I've got a great relationship with Derby as a club and the rest of the fans there.

I had no doubt that Stoke would be among the contenders to get promoted the following season and like all of the players there, the Premier League was where I wanted to be. That said, we've seen so often in football that you can't bank on the future, you can never be 100 per cent certain, that's why we love the game.

What was certain was that I was enjoying playing some of the best football of my career and was club captain of a squad that I was immensely proud to be a part of, never mind lead.

13

Back With Roy

Given the way things were going, the last thing on my mind was leaving Stoke City. Even when I was informed by my agent just before I went on my summer holiday that Sunderland had made an enquiry, I didn't pay it much consideration as I thought the club might just turn down the offer – and I was happy with that, at first.

After I came back from holiday I was driving somewhere and listening to the local radio. Stoke have got an online message board called 'the Oatcake' and someone had posted that they'd been on holiday in the same area as me and that he'd heard me telling my dad about Sunderland's interest.

That provoked quite a bit of debate and was picked up by the radio. One of the directors, Tony Scholes, was on the show and one of the first questions he was asked was about the rumours surrounding my future. Instead of rubbishing it, Tony confirmed there was an interest from Sunderland. For me, that was a shock, but a clear indication that the club were obviously willing, or looking, to sell me. I called him afterwards and he said we should meet up for a coffee. He confirmed at the meeting that Sunderland were interested and asked my thoughts. I said, honestly, that it wasn't about money, and that obviously my ambition was to play in the Premier League. He said he understood and it almost seemed as if he was willing me to go – the conversation ended with him saying he'd keep me in the loop regarding the negotiations.

Sunderland, under Roy Keane, were spending quite a lot of money on their return to the Premier League. They made a couple of offers for me, money plus players, and those offers were rejected.

As the season got underway, there was no suggestion that the move was close to happening. For me, I had to be professional under the circumstances. But I'll be honest and say that, by now, I did want to move. It wasn't that I necessarily wanted to leave Stoke as I'd loved my time there, I just had my head turned by the prospect of playing in the Premier League and not having to wait a year.

As strong as my relationship was with Tony Pulis I was also attracted to the prospect of playing under Roy, who had been such an incredible player and, of course, someone I'd spent time with at United. Tony had a different view to the board and said that he didn't want me to go. I understood but expressed what an opportunity it was – I asked him to consider any reasonable offers, and he said he would.

My agent was in dialogue with Tony and the same kind of things were repeated – a reasonable offer would be accepted but not encouraged as Tony's preference was to keep hold of me. Strangely, the next we heard was Tony Scholes calling my agent to offer me a new contract. I was offered the same amount of money with a clause that said if I left in January instead, I'd get 10 or 15 per cent of any transfer fee. For me, that just reinforced the impression that Scholes felt I should go and that it was only a matter of if, and not when. With that in mind, I thought it might be better to go sooner rather than later.

Still, I maintained my professionalism and was happy to play. I was in the team for the opening game against Cardiff which saw us get a great 1-0 win and then I was in the side that suffered a League Cup exit against Rochdale. It's often been erroneously stated that I didn't play in that game, that I'd refused or feigned an injury to get out of it, but I did play – I couldn't understand where that myth has come from. I did get injured in the game and had to come off after about 40 minutes – I missed the next game at home to Charlton and then the team went to South-ampton.

The manager asked me how I was and I said I wasn't fit to play, though I travelled down there with him still trying to convince me. I didn't have an issue with that – he'd convinced me to play through pain in the past and most of the time I'd got through those games okay, but on this occasion, I just wasn't right. Tony got a bit annoyed and started saying that the move to Sunderland would still go through if I played, but it wasn't about the move, I just wasn't quite fit.

I was stood outside the dressing room when George Burley saw me and came over to talk. He asked how I was and asked if the reason I wasn't playing was because I was moving – I insisted that my ankle was still too sore.

Following the game, Tony was interviewed saying that the rumours were true and I was soon to be on my way.

Those quotes made it into the Sunday papers the day after which I read as I went into the club to have some treatment on my ankle. But while the speculation grew, there still seemed to be no actual movement until the next day when Sunderland put in a bid of around £2.5 million. I thought it was ridiculous money – I'd only cost Stoke £225,000 the year before. Okay, that was money they were willing to pay, so that's their call, but it still seemed a lot – I felt reassured that the size of the bid meant that Stoke were likely to see it as a good deal, too, one good for all parties.

Tony said to my agent that I could go, but that he'd lost a bit of respect for me. He also said that I could only leave on the condition that I submitted an official transfer request to him and Peter Coates, so the next morning I got to the stadium and found two envelopes. I scribbled something down with my reasoning on it. I went to the manager's office, where he was sat with John Rudge. He was nice and civil with me as we said our goodbyes.

Alex Black was my agent and had looked after me for a couple of years after the previous nightmares. He stayed my agent until the day I retired and I've had many reasons to be thankful to him for his help. This was one such occasion. He travelled with me to Sunderland and we stayed in a hotel where I was due to meet Roy Keane in the morning.

Early next morning, I called Alex to say I wasn't sure whether I actually wanted to move – I had got cold feet because of how well everything had gone for me at Stoke, and I was uncertain whether or not the strange feeling I had was a discomfort telling me that I didn't really want to sign.

Alex reassured me that it was a good opportunity and that although what I was feeling was genuine, it was probably due to the fact I'd had such a good time at the club. There was nothing wrong with that, but the chance to work with Roy at Sunderland was too good to turn down. That reasoning calmed me down a little as I agreed to go to the training ground to meet Roy and have lunch with him – it was a chance for us to talk alone as the rest of the players had the day off following a League Cup defeat the night before.

The time I spent with Roy, and a couple of conversations later with Alex, convinced me it was the right move, and as I agreed to sign, I learned that Kenwyne Jones was also being bought for £6m. I thought it was a lot of money but as soon as I saw him on the pitch I realised he was worth every penny.

Sunderland weren't the only team spending big – United had just won the league for the first time in four years and had reinforced a strong squad with the signings of Owen Hargreaves, Carlos Tevez, Nani and Anderson. As luck would have it, they were the first team I would face at Sunderland – at Old Trafford. In all honesty, it was probably a good time to play them as they had a few injuries and were still finding their rhythm.

We stayed in the Worsley Marriott before the game and Roy being Roy sat us through a video and went through every one of their players. "He's weak, he's not the player he used to be," that kind of thing. It was clear Roy wanted us to be robust and show that those who were writing us off before the game were wrong. He told our lads to go in hard on challenges and let them know we were there whenever we got the chance. Anderson and Nani were new to the English game and Roy wanted us to give them the kind of the introduction that he would – hard, but fair. It rubbed off on us, too, as we gave a really good account of ourselves. United won 1-0 but they had to work hard for it – I was given man of the match by our local paper in Sunderland.

There are many things that I'll say about Roy which will obviously give an insight into him as a manager but the first thing to say is that despite the fact we'd played well, he was disappointed we hadn't got a result at Old Trafford. That was typical of him. Yes, of course, we all probably felt we were a little unfortunate but as the season wore on I got the impression that Roy found it difficult to accept that players couldn't do what he could do. Who could? In my lifetime, he's simply one of the best midfielders I've had the pleasure of either seeing, playing with or playing against.

We won our next game, against Reading, and I felt I did well again – Kenwyne certainly did, scoring a belting goal. While Roy was happy with the win, he said we should have won by four – that was him all over. We drew 2-2 at Middlesbrough before a defeat at home to Blackburn and I must admit to making a mistake that cost us in that game. I played a short ball and Roque Santa Cruz scored from it – that really damaged my confidence a bit.

Our routine in the week was that we would play 11 v 11 on Thursdays and then five-a-sides on Fridays. Whenever Roy joined in, he was the best player on the pitch, still, by a country mile. The sessions were intense and he would love it when players would go flying into tackles. He accepted players would fall out and encouraged us to be open about that.

There was a time at the start of the '08/09 season after we'd just signed Pascal Chimbonda that we were doing heading practice in training. He had just had his hair done in braids and refused to head the ball. I was a bit annoyed by that and I don't think I was the only one. At the end of the session, Roy pulled us all together. He had noticed the tension.

"Lads, listen, if any of you have a problem with each other, don't hold back, just get it out. I won't fine youse or nothing, if someone has something to say, that's just how it is. Say it."

No holds barred – just as he was a player. I'll be the first to admit that I did find that environment a little difficult as I'm not that kind of person but then, Roy is a very unique character in his own way and not many are like him, are they? That honest attitude summed up the winner he was.

I didn't particularly play well in a 1-0 defeat at Manchester City which preceded the North East derby at our place in November, 2007. I was going to be dropped, no doubt about it, I could tell that by the fact I wasn't in what looked like the 'first team' in the 11 v 11 on the Thursday. Of course I was gutted, no-one likes to be dropped, but I especially didn't want to miss the derby.

On Friday, it was the usual five-a-side. We didn't do anything else. It would be full-on and Roy, more often than not, would pick his team based on how they performed in that. In this particular game, I scored a hat-trick and come Saturday I'm in the team. It's blatantly obvious that I've been picked on the back of this training session. I scored in the derby, and Roy admitted afterwards that he selected me because of my hat-trick and he fancied me to get a goal. He made a call that I would benefit from the momentum gained by that five-a-side display.

There was a method to what Roy was doing and for me it certainly influenced my attitude to train with just as much intensity as I would if I was playing. Roy didn't care for egos or if someone had played brilliantly the week before. If that player was tossing it off in training, they weren't going to be considered. It was a higher standard that was expected and that standard was expected at all times. You have to respect that kind of approach because it's for the best of the club and it gives everyone an equal chance.

Nonetheless, of course, I'm aware that people have been sceptical of Roy's management. I hope people judge me on how I behave and interact with them, not on the stories they've heard from others, because that's how I judge others. It's the same with Roy. People who don't know him personally have plenty of negative things to say about him but he had been nothing but an inspiration to me.

I'd observed him at close quarters as a player and even though I felt that it was a lot of money, I can't put into words the amount of pride I felt that Roy was willing to bring me to his club. I'd also like to give myself some credit here and think that he'd seen something in my ability and mentality that made him think I was the right kind of player to help him build a successful team. I certainly wasn't the only former United player he had in the ranks and I would like to think that he looked at the players he had known previously and thought there were no heirs or graces about us. What I also think this proved is that the perception of bitterness which he allegedly harboured for United was wide of the mark.

There was myself, Liam Miller, Paul McShane, Kieran Richardson, as well as more senior players like Dwight Yorke and

Andy Cole. You can question the varying degrees of ability within that group but at that time we'd all run through brick walls for Roy and that was what he wanted.

It was a calculated risk he'd taken in acknowledging that we'd been brought up the right way, not only in a footballing sense but also in terms of our lifestyle. I don't know how much Roy would like to acknowledge it, but it seemed to me that it was very much something he'd learned from Sir Alex and that's anything but a bad thing.

The Newcastle result had been decent but it was in a run of results that were far from it – six defeats in nine games before we played Aston Villa was enough to tell us that. That game was the scene of one of the most bizarre team talks I've ever experienced, and that's saying something from someone who had a childhood acquaintance give one. It was bizarre at the time, but turned out to be a stroke of genius.

"Listen lads," he said. "Basically, you're shit. Try and enjoy the game. You're probably going to get beat. But just enjoy being shit."

Then he just walked out. Those words have got to be insulting to any professional no matter who they come from and I'll admit it served as perfect motivation to get out there and prove him wrong. I scored after ten minutes, and we were leading at half-time. We ended up drawing.

It was a decent result, Villa were doing okay and Roy's reverse psychology had worked – on me, at least, for definite. He's a far more clever person than people realise or would like to acknowledge. He knew what he was doing when he said that, he knew the reaction he would get from some of us, and that was a trick right out of the Brian Clough handbook. No doubt about it. That sort of thing was used at United, too. Jim Ryan used to give me so much shit, he was always on my back. On at me every single day, even when I'd not done anything wrong. When someone else had done something wrong, I got the shit for it.

Shortly after my debut against Leicester, after training, Jim said, "Come on Danny, get in the car with me" to go over from the Cliff to Littleton Road. He asked me what I made of my full debut and I confessed I loved it, absolutely loved it. Feeling bold, I said "Can I ask you something?"

"Of course you can, Danny."

"Why are you always on at me? Every day since I've been an apprentice. It's just stick even when I haven't done anything wrong as you always bring it back to me, and honestly, it does feel like you bullied me a bit."

"Listen Danny, here's a bit of advice for you. It'll do you the world of good. If people have a go and they're on at you like that, it's because they like you. You probably won't find it in any walk of life other than football but it's true. The time to really be worried is when it stops, because then no-one wants to know you, they've given up on you."

It's a piece of advice I took with me and passed on to young lads as well. Not exactly conventional but these are the things that sometimes make the difference in a sporting environment, particularly football, and it's better to give some kids a heads-up to let them know. Roy had done something similar before the Villa game but Tony Pulis was particularly brilliant at it, always knowing the right time to have a dig.

Roy was probably well within his rights to have a go at us before the Villa game as we'd not long been given a hiding which was one of the lowest points of my career. We went to Everton, and started quite well, but were soon chasing the game and just kept letting goals in. It was mistake after mistake. It ended up 7-1.

I was living by myself in an apartment in Durham – I was supposed to be going out for Marlon Broome's 30th birthday in Manchester later that day but I couldn't bring myself to go. I took that Everton defeat personally as I was a part of that defence and I felt awful; I didn't have any reason to celebrate. I got back on the bus and went back to Durham. Didn't even open the curtains until Monday morning when I was due to go training. You learn from these kind of occasions – fortunately enough, I never suffered from too many crushing defeats but it teaches you to try and not take the defeats too painfully, just as you don't want to get carried away with a big win. That was something I learned more and more as my career went on.

I was home alone again the day after the Villa game; I got up the next morning but I couldn't walk. I thought I might have slept funny but the pain got worse throughout the day. On Monday morning I went in and explained what was happening and that the pain was coming from my little toe, which was now showing signs of bruising. I went for an X-ray which revealed I'd actually broken it during the game – it had been so cold on that Saturday in December in the North East that when somebody stood on it (and I have no recollection of who did it or how it happened), they must have broken it.

Despite the injury, there was no chance of me missing any games. Roy spoke to me about the situation as we were down to the bare bones in terms of centre halves so he asked me to play through the pain for the next three or four games.

I've always been one to do what I could within my power so throughout this time, I was barely walking, barely doing anything in the gym and just getting by on the painkilling injections on the day of the games. I was used to them anyway as I'd had a few at Stoke.

I don't think I ever learned my lesson because I kept playing on a couple of serious injuries later on when I should just have come off. This was a smaller sacrifice but Roy appreciated it – I got through a couple of games and got us into January when we were able to bring in Jonny Evans on loan from United.

Roy called me into his office to thank me and give me some time off. It was a well needed opportunity to spend time with the family.

14

Great Expectations

I was a good, dependable professional, and if there was any doubt at all about that, I'd proven it to Roy with my attitude and sacrifice playing through the pain.

After my short break I started going into the club to begin treatment. On one of these days, my journey into the club was disrupted bizarrely when a huge fire broke out on the main road after an accident involving a lorry. It was carrying pigs – they were everywhere. I called the club, concerned that I'd be late. "No worries," I was told. I did get there late but only by a minute at 9.01am.

The lads who were injured were expected to turn up early

so the physios could look at them before they worked with the first team. It just so happened that, on this day, Roy had called a meeting with some of the injured lads to address the fact that some of them had been late. Just my luck. Roy was alright with me but was in full cry when I got there. "When youse are injured you're no good to me so you get yourself fit and you will be," he was saying.

Fair enough, and he had a point in what he said. The physios had work schedules to organise and us arriving early was a part of that. A few of the lads protested, Roy's response was: "Set off earlier, then." He came to me and I explained that I did set off early, there was just nothing I could do. "Okay," Roy said, "Don't worry about it."

Next day, I got back to my apartment and there was a letter from the club. It was a massive fine! I spent some time wondering about whether I should appeal or not and in the end decided to accept it.

I continued my way back to fitness and that included a game for the reserves against Manchester City – myself, Ian Harte and a couple of other lads hoping to make our way back into the first team played against a fairly strong side featuring plenty of senior players. We lost 1-0 in front of Roy and on the bus on the way back we're told the manager has set up a meeting to speak to us all the next morning. We got there early, a mix of us senior lads and a few younger lads who had only recently been told they wouldn't be getting their contracts renewed. Roy came in.

"First of all lads, last night was fucking unacceptable."

Personally, I didn't think it was too bad a performance considering we had some young lads in the side. Holding back is the last thing on Roy's mind at this point, and he went round us individually, addressing the kids first.

"You've got to start applying yourselves in games. You've got to give everything. If you carry on like last night, you'll find yourselves working at fucking Sainsbury's this time next year. You'll be on the dole," he's growling. Gets to me. "Danny," he says, "All I'm fucking hearing from you when I'm watching that game yesterday is fucking encouragement. That's all I'm hearing." I thought, well, that's not so bad. "I don't fucking want that. I want you to tell some of them they're being c**ts. Tell them." It wasn't in my nature – I wasn't going to do that, but equally, I wasn't going to bite back at Roy. I was close to making my return and didn't want to put it in any risk. To me, even through the hard words he had said, I could see there was a genuine compassion from Roy for these kids. Even though they didn't have a future at Sunderland, he wanted them not to waste the talent they did have.

I was back in the first team after about a month out for a game at Derby on March 1st – we drew 0-0, and towards the end of the game I had a chance to get the win. It was a difficult one – I thought I did well to connect with it at full stretch, and the keeper did equally well to pull off a save. Roy wasn't happy afterwards.

"Fucking hell, Danny, how did you miss that?" he questioned. Maybe he was right, I thought – maybe I could have done better. I watched the highlights later and thought, you know, I've done alright there. It was unlucky. Monday morning, to be fair, Roy pulled me over in the warm-up.

"Listen Danny, I saw that chance again – it was a tough one. I apologise, I was wrong," he admits.

Fair play to him. That was the other side to those who insist he's rash, unfair, irrational – he approached me when he probably didn't need to. A matter of principle.

I was in and out of the team after my return but was included for the win over Middlesbrough which guaranteed our safety – furthermore, I got one of our goals in the 3-2 win. In the next game, our penultimate one of the season, we lost at Bolton 2-0. Roy came in after the game and the mood around the dressing room was essentially, 'Ok, we've lost, we could have done better, but we've just secured our safety'. Roy went ballistic – scary at the time, but looking back, another indicator of his standards and expectations for the club.

"You're the reason I'm driving up and down the fucking country to find another player, you're not fucking good enough," he yells at one player. "Your attitude is shit. You're not good enough," he bawls at others.

"Next week we've got our last home game, against Arsenal. You know at the end of the season when you walk around the pitch, thank the fans for their support? I'm ringing Umbro, and getting you some hooded jumpers, because you're a fucking embarrassment, it's a joke and this is not going to stay this way," he finishes.

I was taken aback. That was the time when I really began to believe that his expectations for us were simply much too high. It's not just something with Roy, it's something I've noticed with other great players who have gone into management, with Glenn Hoddle for example. I imagine Bryan Robson was the same too. Bryan did well at Middlesbrough but never quite as well as some expected (or should it be said, that's the perception, because I think he did well there).

New direction: The lure of working with Roy Keane as a boss took me to Sunderland in 2007

Defender's nightmare: Being back in the Premier League meant I had my hands full keeping an eye on the likes of Michael Owen (right). One of my first tests was coming up against a new-look United team including Anderson

Head boy: A training ground hat-trick earned me a place in the team and Roy's selection decision was justified when I scored against Newcastle

Home, where the heart is: On the run against Everton in September, 2008 (left). It was good to get back in the dressing room and pull on my old shirt

Photo courtesy of Phil Greig

Tunnel vision: Leading out the team and looking focused ahead of an important game against Blackburn. It was Tony Pulis's 300th match in charge – we won 3-0 and I scored

On the mark: Celebrating after scoring the first goal in a 2-0 win over Bolton in January, 2011. The atmosphere at the Britannia was always a bit special

Higgy in the middle: In the centre circle before we knocked Arsenal out of the FA Cup with a 3-1 win. Their attitude grated on me whenever we played them

On the march: The free-kick that took us to Wembley in the FA Cup semi-final against West Ham in 2011 (above). Top: The celebration wasn't planned – and I'm not sure what Rory is doing! Left: Delight after the final whistle

Key to success: The fans sum up the way they feel about Tony 'the messiah' Pulis

As good as it gets: Full of confidence thanks to our FA Cup run, I scored a free-kick as we demolished Newcastle 4-0 at the Brit (above). I felt on top of the world (left). Little did I know what was around the corner…

Do it for Danny: Signing autographs for the fans on FA Cup final day. Seeing their banners meant so much – but I just didn't want to be there

Beginning of the end: The injury every footballer dreads – the cruciate (inset, right). Below: I made my return against Maccabi Tel Aviv and my final game for Stoke was against Besiktas, also in the Europa League   *Photo courtesy of Phil Greig*

Proud day: Lining up in Portugal for Gibraltar's first recognised international against Slovakia, which ended in a 0-0 draw. I class this as one of my greatest football achievements

On the road: I had spells at (from left) Ipswich Town, Nottingham Forest and Sheffield United. But deep down I knew I was coming to the end of my career

Second chance: Doing some punditry work for BT Sport. Starting a new career in the media gave me the same buzz as playing

Next generation: I'm so proud of my fantastic children – Jak, Jessica, Joshua and Jacob

Looking ahead, not back: There is plenty of road left to travel...

Photo: Tony Woolliscroft

A lot of players who aren't playing at the absolute highest level sometimes need things repeating, they need repetition whereas for the best, they don't. Those things come naturally. Like I said, Roy was still better than anyone in training. If he wanted to put his boots back on he'd have undoubtedly walked straight into the side and not just because he was picking it. He'd smash the ball at us in training to test our touch. I'd think, "Alright, I'll do it back to you" – he'd kill it, an immaculate first touch.

At all the clubs I'd been at previously there were differing end of season bonuses, bonuses for staying up or getting in the top half. At Sunderland – who had just been promoted – there was only a bonus for getting into the top ten.

Again, that was Roy's mentality. And it had nothing to do with money. He thought that was the least he should expect from us, but he was used to the very best, and with all due respect to our squad, it was optimistic to suggest we should finish in the top half. I'm not saying we weren't given generous bonuses besides – our appearance bonus and win bonus was great, but the main one was that top half bonus which never really seemed remotely achievable.

Maybe if I'd have been younger, it would have been a perfect situation for me, but particularly coming off the back of such a wonderful time at Stoke, it never quite felt right. That's not down to Roy, it's just me. Regardless of what anyone says about him or might read into from the examples and stories I've shared, high standards can never be a bad thing for a club.

It's not all about where you are at the time and as dedicated as I was to the cause, I'd been missing Stoke – in fairness I had been after only a month or so of my time at Sunderland. That's meant with no disrespect to Sunderland or the fans but I'd enjoyed my year at Stoke more than anywhere else and while I could never say Tony wasn't as ambitious as Roy, perhaps the standards they set weren't quite the same. I don't think I was the only one at Sunderland struggling with that.

My old pal Scouse was holding fitness sessions in the summer, primarily for the Stoke lads to do a bit of running – though it was not officially connected to the club in any way, it was just an informal thing.

I went and joined in and got talking to the players again and it began to make me think that if I could go back there, I could enjoy my football as much as I did when I was last there. Tony Pulis had been in touch a couple of times with my agent on an informal basis and we'd managed to move on from any lingering ill will that might have existed after my move – so much so, in fact, that he told me he would love to bring me back. He wasn't the only one who wanted to sign me. Mick McCarthy at Wolves put in an offer to Sunderland, which was rejected.

The offer was enough to prompt Roy to ask to see me – he told me about the bid, but that it wasn't enough. He said if an offer came in that was good enough, he wouldn't stand in my way but I was still at the club at the start of the next season.

We played against Sporting Lisbon in a friendly. In their team was the former Middlesbrough midfielder Fabio Rochemback. He was getting a little bit lively, a little bit rowdy in this game and when Grant Leadbitter tried to get past him, Rochemback went straight through Grant.

Grant was just a young lad and I thought it was a really nasty challenge so I confronted Fabio. Next thing, Roy came on and dragged me away, but I could tell that he was buzzing with what I'd done.

After the game he said to me, "I've got no issues with you doing that, sticking up for your team, no problems at all."

That commitment wasn't enough to get me a starting spot for our first game of the 2008/09 season against Liverpool at home. I was on the bench. We lost 1-0 and then travelled to Tottenham.

Before the game, we went for a walk – the team had already been named. Pascal Chimbonda and Carlos Edwards had been named in the team but turned up late for the walk. We don't think anything of it, but Keane notices everything. When we get to the ground, Keane's addressing the team and says "Right, Pascal, Carlos, you're not fucking playing. If you can't turn up on time for a walk then you're not playing today, you're not in the squad." This isn't a run of the mill game and these aren't run of the mill players for Sunderland – he'd only just bought Pascal. He didn't care. That was good to see, in a way, that he had those principles – and it was good for me as I started, and we won 2-1. Roy's decision justified.

With no move on the horizon, my only thoughts were staying in the team. Our next game was against Nottingham Forest in the League Cup, and I was back on the bench. With all the changes and goings-on at the club I was led to believe by these decisions that I wasn't part of Roy's first eleven and so I thought that a move would be better in any event.

I was on the bench, unused as a substitute again, for the defeat against Manchester City, and the next day my agent rings me up to tell me Tony Pulis is coming in for me. "He's left it as long as possible as he feels Sunderland do want you to go but he thinks he might get a better price," he says. I was due to play for the reserves the next day but was contacted by someone at the club to tell me a bid had been put in. In all honesty, I wasn't only glad but I was grateful to Sunderland that they weren't standing in my way.

It seemed like a straightforward deal to me, and it was only later I found out that the negotiations were somewhat protracted between Roy and Tony. Roy was adamant that Sunderland wanted the same money they paid for me – Tony baulked at the price. "Why?" asked Roy. Tony replied: "I told you in the first place, he's not worth that amount of money!" In the end, I think Sunderland had agreed a deal to pay Stoke in instalments so they agreed to just waive the outstanding money and that became my transfer fee, something around £2m. And with that, the love affair I'd begun two years prior resumed.

Roy walked out of Sunderland a couple of months later and had a relatively short spell at Ipswich Town before accepting a role as Martin O'Neill's assistant for the Republic of Ireland and Paul Lambert's right hand man at Aston Villa.

I think his spell at Sunderland is sometimes unfairly undervalued, or written off as unsuccessful, when in actual fact he did very well there.

Why do I think he hasn't yet quite been a manager at the highest level? I think there are too many egos in the modern game that need stroking. Some don't react that well to Roy's style of management. If you've got a squad of 24 or 25, a third might be egos, another third might be players who react well to Roy's style, and then the remaining third might well be players who go into their shell in reaction to that style. It is difficult in the modern era for managers at the highest level and that's why I believe one of, if not *the* single most important ability they need to have is unbelievable man-management.

It's a different generation now. There are still old school players of course but there are too many who react to comments personally. That's why it's vital, too, to have a great assistant – every world class manager has a fantastic number two, someone the manager and the players can trust in confidence.

Looking back at my time with Sunderland, I felt I struggled, for whatever reason. I would put it down to under-performance. People afterwards have tried to reassure me, the Sunderland fans have always been fantastic with me and told me I did well and scored some vital goals, but I always felt like I didn't do myself justice. In hindsight, I feel that is partly down to the fact that I felt I let Roy down. I couldn't meet his standards. I have no-one else to blame but myself. I played for a lot of managers who had different techniques and ideas. As a footballer you're paid to do as the manager asks and deal with the environment. I didn't, as much as I wanted to.

That said, I don't regret my year at Sunderland. I was delighted to have played under Roy – it was a learning curve for me. I was able to see that he was equally motivated as a manager as he was as a player and in some of the methods he used I gained insight into why he was that way. He was so driven it was unbelievable – I thought I was, but he was on another level.

One thing's for sure, of the many privileges I've had throughout my career, the honour of playing with, playing against, being bought by and then being managed by Roy Keane is one of the most rewarding experiences I've ever had.

15

Going Home

I've tried to avoid cliches where possible but they're probably unavoidable when it comes to describing my return to Stoke City. It did feel like going home, it did feel so right. I enjoyed myself just about wherever I'd been but I did honestly feel like that first year at Stoke had been the time I'd felt like I most belonged. In that respect, I have to give a lot of credit to Tony Pulis for playing his part in the resolution of our friendship. He could've binned me off. He didn't have to make any kind of effort to bring me back to Stoke but I was so glad he did.

Being completely honest, in those later days at Sunderland when I was beginning to wonder whether it was right for me there, I did feel more than just a tinge of jealousy watching the lads at Stoke get promoted to the Premier League.

As the season got underway, I was keeping a close eye on their fortunes – not only because I was being linked with a return, but because of the relationships I'd built up in my previous spell there. Stoke lost their first game, 3-1 at Bolton, and one of the bookmakers paid out on them being relegated. Tony loved that, it was all the fuel he needed to instil the underdog spirit around the club. A week later they recorded a memorable win over Aston Villa in their first home game – and a week after that, I was on my way back.

It was an uncertain time before I'd signed; I was waiting with the phone in my hand on transfer deadline day just hoping that a move to Stoke would come off. The call did come in the end and when I got back, it really was like I'd never been away.

I don't say this lightly but standing in the tunnel at the Britannia before a game sent shivers down my spine; how 27,000 people could generate such an atmosphere was unbelievable. I'd been in stadiums with twice that many who generated less. The lead-up to home games was incredible. I'd love it. Getting there before a game, I would be itching to get ready and go out to warm up, just to be a part of that atmosphere. Opposition teams wouldn't know what hit them, particularly in that first season in the Premier League, and I think a lot of times we won games before the first whistle was even blown.

I was given quite a welcome back by those fans. They had always been great towards me, but I wasn't quite sure how they might react considering the way I'd left the club the first time around.

I'd signed on deadline day and there were no games for a couple of weeks because of the international break, so Tony asked me to play in a reserve game to get my fitness up. It was against Villa and they moved the game to the Brit. There was an unusually large crowd, and I realised that they'd come for me. I scored in the game, to make it even better.

It wasn't quite the same fairytale ending for my first senior game back, at home to Everton. We lost 3-2 and I was at fault for the deciding goal. Still, to step out in front of such a crowd – I'd never seen it full before – was incredible. When I got home that evening, everything couldn't have felt more right.

The following week we played at Liverpool in what was arguably the most incredible 0-0 game I've been involved in. How we got a draw and a clean sheet I don't know. They had a goal disallowed after about a minute, and honestly, if that hadn't have been ruled out it would probably have been a cricket score.

Ibrahima Sonko had to go off because he'd been smashed in the face with the ball. That was typical of our performance – bodies everywhere – so to walk off the pitch with a point was a big statement for us. I don't think we got out of our half but it showed that we could somehow get results. In the dressing room afterwards I think the general mood was one of disbelief; keeping them out at the Kop end in the second half was a real effort. I'd won there before with Southampton but this felt like a bigger achievement, against a Liverpool side that was probably the best it had ever been in the Premier League.

The following week we were defeated at home by a very strong Chelsea side. I was playing left back, and in the build-up, Tony pulled me to one side and asked if I would go tight on their winger, Florent Malouda. We were beaten 2-0 but Tony was happy with my performance – he said he'd noticed that I didn't go tight on Dirk Kuyt the previous week. Kuyt was more workmanlike than Malouda and although some might say that they find the more hard working players more difficult to play against, for me it was the tricky, quick wingers every time. I consider myself quick, or not slow for that point, but it was always tougher coming up against someone who was known for getting in behind. For that reason and the fact that Tony had been so forthcoming in his praise, I was very happy with how I'd done against Malouda despite the fact that we'd lost. At 29, I was still learning 'new tricks', ways of progressing my game, and that was down to what Tony saw in me.

We lost at Portsmouth which meant that the good result at Liverpool was sandwiched by two defeats either side. Being perfectly honest, we were looking at our home form rather than our away form as being the crucial factor in our attempt to stay in the top flight.

Our pitch was as small as it could possibly be under the regulations to suit the way that Tony liked to play. We could leave certain positions free and compensate by moving around quickly in a unit. On the bigger pitches away from home, we would use the same tactics but find ourselves isolated. It also meant that we could bully teams and get in their face at home.

After two defeats from our first three home games, however, we had to start delivering.

Tom Soares – as well as Michael Tonge – signed on the same day as I did and Tom helped make the breakthrough in our next game, at home to Spurs following the second international break. Soaresy had bags of talent and he was brilliant in this game – he caused them no end of problems, getting the man of the match. He was responsible for getting us a penalty when Gareth Bale, of all people, brought him down and was sent off.

This was when Bale was playing left back and, at the time, was considered something of a bad luck charm to Tottenham who hadn't won with him in the side. Unthinkable, when you look at what he did afterwards.

As I'd taken spot-kicks in the Championship, there wasn't really any argument from anyone when I stepped up to take the penalty this time around. I put the ball on the spot and turned my back to walk away.

When I turned to face it, the ball had rolled off the spot. Even most neutrals will be aware that the Britannia can be the home of bad weather conditions and on this day, the wind was terrible. I put the ball on the spot again and when I turned back around, it had rolled off again. The third time, the ball stayed still, and I took a step back, about to start my run up. All went quiet in the stadium...

The ball rolled off the spot again.

There was a huge groan. The tension had become almost tangible. I'm reminding myself that I need to be the calmest man in the stadium and not change my mind about where I plan to put it. The Spurs fans behind the goal are loving it.

At this point, it's not even about the game anymore, not about the result. I feel like it's just me against this fucking football, a battle of wits between us. Thankfully, it stays on the spot the fourth time, I hit it and Gomes goes the right way but the strike goes past him into the corner. It was relief rather than joy with which I celebrated that one!

It's almost all for nothing as five minutes later Darren Bent equalises. Then, though, comes the turning point. Everyone is aware by now of what we would do at throw-ins – Rory would take them and we'd set up a crowd scene in the box to cause havoc. I'd rarely be a part of that. I'd either be loose, a decoy or someone Rory would use to get the ball back from. We're launching a few of these throws-in to the box and Gomes is hating every minute of it – one time he gets cleaned out and is so upset he looks like he's in tears.

It all adds to the pressure and Rory himself scores early in the second half but the action is far from over – Alan Hutton fouls Thomas Sorensen which means our keeper has to be brought off. That cranks the atmosphere up another notch and then Soares wins another penalty – I let Ricardo take this one, but he hits both posts and Rory skies the rebound. Afterwards, Ricardo and I strike a deal – I would take all the penalties except for the ones that he wins himself.

Spurs get another man sent off near the end and that's just enough to help us over the line and get a massive win. In just a few weeks at the start of the 2008/09 season I'd beaten Spurs twice! That was the end of Juande Ramos, who'd overseen a terrible start to the season for them, and he was replaced by Harry Redknapp. That was the start of great things at the club. The atmosphere at that game – though I keep going on about it – was fantastic, it really was. The game was live on Sky and shortly afterwards I think they did an audio assessment to test which was the loudest stadium in the Premier League – Stoke was the loudest by a distance.

We did lose our next game, at Manchester City, but managed to get back on track when we welcomed Sunderland to the Brit. Midway through the second half, I went up for a challenge with Steed Malbranque, who'd signed for them in the summer. I didn't have any problems with him in particular but I did find him to be pretty arrogant during training sessions; he'd sneer at things certain players did. If I made a mistake, he'd tut at me almost dismissively.

In this challenge we went up together and he elbowed me in the back of the head. It was intentional, no doubt about it, he should have been sent off. I jumped up and grabbed hold of him by the scruff of the neck. Roy Keane was on the sideline and was shouting at me. It's not in my character but I feel I owe Malbranque one – a few Sunderland players try and calm me down, including Phil Bardsley, who I got on with quite well.

I was fuming, saying that he'd done it on purpose – he's nearly a foot smaller than me and I felt it was a bit of a shithouse tactic. I think to myself that the next time he gets the ball, I'm going to go into him – it's worth a booking.

Sure enough, I soon get an opportunity. I can't even remember if it was a good challenge, all I know is I've gone in hard enough to let him know that I'm there and hopefully hurt him a bit. I walk away as the foul is blown, but I don't get booked.

As I look back, it's Phil Bardsley that I've gone into. I went straight over and apologised and explained – to be fair to Phil, he says 'no problem'. For me, that means I can't really afford to take the chance to go into anyone else. Then Malbranque gets taken off by Roy. Two wrongs don't make a right but I would have had no problems if Bardo had come in and smashed me. We won 1-0 with a goal from Ricardo, so all was well.

I was pleased with my own performances, happy that I was able to keep up a consistent level despite some personal problems. I was going through a split with my partner who I'd had my first two children with and was spending some of my time living in hotels. Out of respect for my kids, I don't really want to go through the gory details. It was a mutual split.

Suffice it to say that I was confident that I was able to concentrate on my football enough for it not to affect my performance, and it has to be said that maybe the distraction helped. Going on the pitch became my oasis, my chance to forget about everything beyond those white lines.

After a victory over Arsenal, we only managed to register one more win in the next nine games – a run in which we faced, and lost to Manchester United twice, though the game against them on Boxing Day was the perfect example of what I said about a top team coming and attempting to match us or roll with it. United won 1-0 with a very late goal and it was seen as a turning point for their season – it was the start of a pretty memorable and hectic Christmas period.

We took on Liverpool early in the New Year in a game that was probably most remembered for the pre-match 'rant' by Rafael Benitez, which had nothing to do with us and everything to do with Sir Alex Ferguson.

Liverpool were flying at the time but Ferguson had got under Benitez's skin and provoked him into such a response. Without a shadow of a doubt, it was a tactic that was worth points. Worth points to United, and at the time, worth points to Stoke City. We drew the game 0-0 and I've since spoken with Liverpool fans who are certain that if they'd won that game they would have benefited from the momentum and gone on to win the league. To get two scoreless draws against them was a great result and a good one for United, too – even though I confess to being a United fan, their fortunes were not on my mind as we battled away to try and gain another valuable point.

After the United game, we'd played West Ham away. We took

an early lead at Upton Park but Carlton Cole equalised and Ricardo Fuller started having an argument with Andy Griffin, basically blaming him for the goal. Nothing out of the ordinary there, that's happened plenty of times over the years, but then they get closer to each other and Ricardo slaps Andy in the face. Ricardo was sent off for his actions and that wound me up as it sort of justified the comments that some people had been making about Stoke and our 'physical' approach to games. But it just wasn't us. Ricardo and Griff were two very passionate players and that situation had boiled over. Sadly it was in front of everyone and didn't help our reputation.

Tony, though, dealt with it brilliantly. His man-management skills with Ricardo had always been spot on – an arm around the shoulder was the way to get the best out of him. Ricardo was a player capable of outrageous moments which saved us on many occasions. The following season, ironically enough against West Ham in a game that was a hell of a battle, he scored an amazing goal. Got the ball on the left hand side, nut-megged one, turned Matty Upson inside out and belted it in. Then nonchalantly goes off like he does it all the time. He's got legendary status at Stoke and rightly so, the lads loved him.

After the red card, he got showered and got straight on the bus. I approached him afterwards and said, "You can't do that mate. We're in a situation where we're scrapping and we need you." Tony called a meeting afterwards to discuss it. Ricardo knew he was in the wrong, but we didn't want to quell his passion either..

I'd still been happy with my own contribution during this period and so was the manager. He pulled me to one side and said, "Danny, you know Ashley Cole, he's the best left back around? I wouldn't swap him for you." I laughed – I knew he probably didn't mean it, but I could see what he was trying to do. To even put me in the same bracket as Cole was ridiculous as he was one of, if not *the* best left back in Europe for a long time. Even though neither me or Tony believed that for one minute, it was a compliment of sorts. Is there any chance he was being genuine? Maybe – in as much as Ashley wouldn't have suited our style of play as much as me, but that's about it!

A couple of days after the Liverpool game we signed James Beattie. From the outside, it might have looked like an insurance policy given what had gone on with Ricardo but I think James would have come in anyway as he was a different kind of player. He was one of the strongest players I'd ever played against or with; a top target man whose finishing ability was up there with other first class strikers.

A lot of the time, Ricardo would set up opportunities and James was the perfect player to act as a foil to Fuller. The previous week we signed Matty Etherington from West Ham and, with James, they were two of the best pieces of business Stoke City ever did. Matty was a fantastic crosser of a ball and was a great signing at just the right time, giving us a new dimension.

We had Mama Sidibe who didn't score plenty of goals but was great at bringing others into play; so the addition of a great crosser and a finisher was perfect. Perhaps the most important thing was that Tony still kept the same philosophy so far as identifying the right kind of players to improve the club, and James and Matty not only brought great quality but they fitted the bill in terms of profile and character too. He could have easily gone out and bought in bigger names, that's always a temptation for teams battling against the drop, but instead of getting players who might give you a nine out of 10 and then a string of four or five out of 10 performances, he wanted players who would give a solid six or seven every week with the potential for the odd eight or nine.

I had the pleasure of playing behind Matty as he and Beats made a dramatic impact on our season; not only was his crossing a new asset for us, but he was also good at carrying the ball 20, 30, 40 yards and relieving the pressure on the defence. A lot of unselfish running, which a more egotistical player might not have done.

From the end of January, we went on a great run of form; we got a good win over Manchester City, and a victory at West Brom where we won 2-0 and I played a part in both goals. Earlier in that game, on about 20 minutes, I went up for a header right in front of the dugout and as I landed I had a massive back spasm. I was in agony. The physio came on and asked if I was alright. I was struggling but I played out the game.

On Monday I went for a scan and discovered I'd given myself two bulging discs in my back. The pain was ridiculous. I didn't train all week, I could barely walk properly. On Friday I hobbled out at the training ground and the lads all said "Danny you can't play," the boss asked me if I could because I was needed and I agreed.

We played against Newcastle, drew 1-1 and I got through it. I was having sugar and water injections in my back. Then I once again had a week free from training before we played Blackburn. In that game, I went up for a header and as I landed I felt such relief, like all the pain had gone in my back, but then all of a sudden I started to experience weird feelings down my right hand side.

My two smallest toes had gone numb; the physio came on and I explained what I was feeling. I could barely walk, but when I ran, the pain went away, so I spent the remainder of the first half running or jogging. At half-time, I laid down on the physio's bed – towards the end of the interval I started feeling shooting pains. They asked if I was right to go back on and I said as long as I could just keep jogging I'd be fine. I played on, and played a part in Liam Lawrence's winning goal.

After the game I was heading down south. I began to drive, and after about an hour I had to stop at the services. I was in so much pain that I was crying. I got down there, eventually, and drove back the next day, but when I got back I could barely move. I had a scan at 8.30am on the Monday – I set off an hour early just to be sure but still didn't make it. I went to training and then straight to the physio room where I immediately assumed the foetal position on the bed.

The physios got everyone out of the room. I was in there with Dave Watson, Chris Banks and Andy Davies, three great physiotherapists and friends. Chris and Andy were wondering what was wrong; they tried to straighten me out but I said if they did that I'd be screaming. It took them over an hour to get me lying flat on my stomach, and after that I didn't want to move. Dave insisted I had to have a scan, which involved a car journey, so he said he'd lay the front seat of the car down.

Once I finally got there and had the scan I was told that one of my discs had exploded. There were bits of my disc pressing against my spine, which was what was causing the pain. I had to go and see a surgeon the next day – I took so many painkillers I could barely tell what day it was. I don't want to be gross, but I had lost control of my bowels as well.

When I saw the surgeon he said he needed to stick a finger up my arse – I thought he was joking! Apparently with some slipped discs if it goes against a certain part of your spine it can cause big problems with regards your nerves and he wanted to see if that was the case, because I might need surgery instantly. It was a good job he did, because I did need the operation soon.

I asked what it entailed and he told me they were going to perform a discectomy – they'd open up my back and clean up the problematic disc parts. My mate Scouse really looked after me at this time and I appreciated it so much; he and his missus Kaz took care of me for quite a while because I couldn't look after myself.

My season was over but I already had to start thinking about rehabilitation throughout the summer. The Blackburn result had more or less meant we were going to stay up but in my absence, the lads won at Hull to guarantee safety. It was a great achievement and I'd like to think that it was the type of character shown by the likes of myself, playing through the pain barrier to give everything for the club and the manager, which made such a difference.

It was the mentality of the club – I would do that for any team, but the entire dressing room felt the same. It was a pleasure to be a part of and it almost felt like a duty and a responsibility to the other lads who gave the same. Sure, it didn't end the greatest way for me that year, but ask me if I'd rewind and do it all again?

You bet I would.

16

Stoke v Arsenal

I worked hard through the summer to get myself into a position where I'd be fit at the start of the 2009/10 season. A typical Tony Pulis pre-season had the emphasis on fitness, so for the best part of the first two weeks we'd not see a ball. Fitness tests for the first few days, then we'd fly out to somewhere like Austria or Switzerland for running and endurance.

The days would consist of running or cycling up mountains. I don't know how he did it, but Tony managed to find steep inclines on the flattest of surfaces. It didn't help that the bikes were old and knackered, with the chains hanging off. Truth be told, the lads were happy when the chains did come off as it meant they didn't have to carry on.

The first few days would be hard, awful – but by the fourth

day, you'd be a zombie, you wouldn't feel any pain in your body. Tony was old school, he wanted to see his players in pain because he knew then you were working hard. We'd be fit, but not football fit, by the time the friendlies came around and that didn't bother Tony one bit as he didn't really care for pre-season. The results didn't matter to him.

That was probably just as well in 2009 as we opened our pre-season campaign with split squads, one playing at Newcastle Town and one at Nantwich Town on the same day. I was in the squad playing at Nantwich and we suffered a 2-0 defeat – it could have been five or six. It wouldn't have been unjust if it was. In the dressing room afterwards we were all thinking about how much grief we were going to get the next day from the other lads but then we found out they lost, too! With two months without kicking a ball, what else could be expected? Once those first few difficult pre-season games were out of the way, we always knew we'd be in a great position to start the league season.

When we weren't being embarrassed in pre-season, the banter around the dressing room was great and spirits were high. One time we went out for a drink and the next morning we called in to training, at a time when we still got changed in Portakabins. Griff and Dave Kitson were changing in different cabins and Kits, who's one of the driest lads you'd ever meet, goes into the one where Griff is and says, "Listen. We went out for a few drinks last night and I just want to say that I don't like you so I don't want anything ever to do with you again. Just keep your distance from me." Griff can be highly strung – Kits just walks off, goes into his cabin and starts to read his paper. Griff is saying, "I'm not putting up with that, I'll have to sort it out."

You can see the newspaper is shaking where Kits is in absolute stitches – he can't hold it in as Griff tries to confront him. Everyone was in hysterics after that. The value in that unity was important in the first season but was vital to how the personality of that Stoke team was shaped for the next few years.

Tony wasn't resting on his laurels ahead of our second season in the Premier League. People speak of the difficulty for promoted teams but how often do you see teams struggle in that second year, trying to replicate the first? It happens for players – Tony Yeboah, Christian Benteke – and teams, like Bradford City and Hull City (back in 2010, as under Steve Bruce they seem to be holding their own). There's always the temptation, which Tony always resisted, to change things in order to advance.

In just one season in the Premier League we'd developed a reputation for being tough to beat and a hard place to visit and that was a huge achievement.

I wouldn't go as far as to say that James Beattie was a perennial sufferer of 'second season syndrome' but the reason he struggled to replicate the success of his first few months was probably due to the increased attention he now faced from opposition defenders. It still worked in our favour, as we had other players free as a consequence. James did have a bit of a falling out with the manager which led to his departure but based on statistics alone, his second season at Stoke is sometimes unfairly regarded as unsuccessful.

We started the season fairly well, setting the trend for the rest of the year. Our August saw two wins and three clean sheets from the first four games. The squad was boosted with the signings of Robert Huth and Tuncay – I didn't see my chances as limited at centre half as I had more often than not played left side anyway. On deadline day, we signed Danny Collins, and it was more his arrival that worried me, as I found myself dropped shortly after.

There was always going to be competition and I got on well with Danny; I didn't mind being dropped, as long as I was given an explanation, and I was a little upset that this time around I wasn't. Instead, I was part of the League Cup team that took part in an eventful game in which we scraped through with a few late goals. We were fortunate to qualify against a strong Blackpool team that went on to get promoted that year.

I wasn't seeing a lot of game time and was in the squad for the next round, at Portsmouth. We flew down, and I'm an awful flyer. Not so bad when it's for the family holiday and you can have a couple of drinks to settle the nerves, but I was unable to this time around. We were destroyed 4-0, fair play, but there were a few of us who hadn't played for a while.

We flew back from Southampton. One of the girls, an employee of the club who organised the travel, always flew with us. She knew how bad I was at flying so was making sure I was alright as we took off. I could smell burning. She was telling me not to be silly, but I told her to check, and she agreed that she could smell it too, so she went and told the pilot. Within 10 minutes we were starting an emergency landing into London. We had to go back by bus, it was about 5am by the time I got to sleep! A disaster of a day.

At least I didn't suffer the embarrassment which Tuncay went through up at Hull – he's a lovely guy and I've got all the time in the world for him but it was never destined to work out for him at Stoke. We were winning 1-0 and he came on; Abdoulaye Faye was sent off and Tuncay was brought straight back off, within about five minutes! You shouldn't, but I was laughing my head off, I couldn't help it. It was typical of his time there.

It wasn't until we played at Aston Villa just before Christmas that I found myself back in the starting line-up, which reminds me of a story. I was a bit hesitant about including this as it doesn't paint me in the best light professionally but here goes…

During my rehab in the summer of 2009 I started seeing an American girl and we decided to get married. That winter, I wanted to go and see her family, to do the right thing and make sure that they'd met me before we tied the knot.

I planned to play the Villa game, fly out on the Sunday, get back on Wednesday and go in to training as normal on Thursday. Of course, I couldn't get the days off in the middle of the season, so I said I was sick. To make it more believable, I pretended to feel unwell on the way to and from Villa. I also arranged with a friend that he would have my mobile, and I got a cheap pay-as-you-go phone that I was going to take to America. If anyone tried to ring me, my friend could let me know, and I could ring up without anyone hearing a ring tone that suggested I was overseas.

I told my parents and they told me I was stupid, not only for the devious way in which I suppose I was planning it, but also because of my career – if I missed a random drugs test and I wasn't at home, that would be one red strike. Three and you're out. I was nervous but I felt that I was doing the right thing. Eventually, my parents saw that I was doing it for the right reasons.

Then the flight got cancelled due to snowstorms in America!

I turned up to training on Monday bright as a button. The lads thought it was a miraculous recovery.

I'd played well at Villa and from that point kept my place – I put in a good performance in a 2-0 defeat at Man City, and we then lost at home to Birmingham in a game where we should have won, but Joe Hart, who was on loan there at the time, put in an exceptional performance.

After the turn of the year, our form gradually picked up. We defeated York in the cup and then faced Fulham at home. At first, we weren't sure whether the game was going to be on as the weather was so bad. It was, and we went into a blistering 3-0 lead – they pulled it back to 3-2 but we held on for a massive three points.

In the following game, we were due to play against Burnley but they got rid of their manager in the week and were hoping the weather would cause a postponement. It did and Tony gave us the weekend off after running the arse off us at the Brit on Friday. Maybe I was feeling guilty for what I'd done before Christmas, but I called up the people who helped me out with travel and said I wanted to take the opportunity to go to America but come back on Sunday. They thought I was crazy, flying there one day just to fly back the next, but I felt it was a matter of principle. It was important for me that I did go out and meet my wife-to-be's parents but equally important that I didn't take advantage of Tony's generosity.

In our next game, in January 2010, Liverpool took advantage of my own generosity, as it was my mistake that let them score – but I atoned for that in the last minute, setting up Huth for the equaliser. We were full of momentum going into our FA Cup game with Arsenal at the Brit and it was another proud moment for me as I was named captain.

It turned into a great day. We absolutely destroyed them – Rory's long throw was put into the net by Ricardo in the first minute and we were better from then until the final whistle. There was no luck or fortune, no question whatsoever that we were completely good value for our comprehensive 3-1 win. Fuller scored again and Dean Whitehead got our other – but at the end of the game, some of the Arsenal players refused to shake our hands. That was disappointing.

I'd not once experienced that, even when I'd played for teams that had beaten Liverpool, Man Utd, Man City and Chelsea. They'd shake hands and wish us the best. Here, Arsenal players basically couldn't accept the result. It was a petulance I'd never come across before and it was completely unnecessary.

For all that was being said and written about our style of play, a fair amount of it could be said to be true. After all, if we'd had gone toe to toe with Arsenal and tried to play the way they did, there would only be one winner. But that's not football – football is about playing to your strengths and ours were getting up in people's faces and being strong but fair.

When we beat Arsenal the previous season, in November 2008, there was an incident when Theo Walcott had to come off – he was racing at such a pace, and Rory and I tried to stop him. Theo buckled under the challenge and I think he had to go off with a dislocated shoulder – no malice, he was just unfortunate. Rory was instrumental in that unlikely win as both of our goals came from long throws.

For all the talk about the exuberance in which we applied our tactics, I'd be surprised if there weren't more Arsenal players sent off than Stoke players in our head to heads in that era. That was the case in that Walcott game – Robin van Persie was dismissed for needlessly barging in on our goalkeeper, Thomas Sorensen.

The attitude of Arsenal grated on me when we played against them. We never got it against any other team. I think if you look back on the period, you might say it reveals more about them than us. Arsene Wenger was outspoken in his criticism but every other manager, be it a top club or a smaller club would say win, lose or draw that they knew how we played and they had to deal with it. We planned to outfight and outmuscle teams and managers like Sir Alex Ferguson, any number of Chelsea managers, any Liverpool manager – they accepted it and set out their sides accordingly.

For some reason, Arsenal would label us as bully boys and rugby players. I've got all the respect and all the time in the world for Wenger and Arsenal but I did find that a little disrespectful. After that game, Arsene claimed the red card for van Persie was harsh while being critical of our approach. At the time, we were too busy celebrating our unlikely victory to really care – but the seeds were sown for a lot of vitriol, undeserved I might add, later down the line.

The big games came thick and fast and Arsenal were due to return for a league game in February a few weeks after the FA Cup tie. Before that, I was forced to come off after tweaking my abductor against Manchester City. The lads managed to get a good result, getting a 1-1 draw.

My injury meant that I was going to miss the game with Arsenal, which I had to watch on television at home. To be fair, they won, 3-1, and were the better team on the day, but the game was overshadowed, of course, by the injury to Aaron Ramsey.

To see any player suffer like that is horrific – thankfully, he's been back a long time and had a great season, probably his best, in 2013/14. It was something you wouldn't wish on anyone and it spoke volumes that Glenn Whelan was one player who was straight by Aaron's side and wanted to be there for him.

Ryan Shawcross, the player involved in the incident which led to Aaron's injury, was distraught. He had been in such a great run of form that he had been called up for England and was due to travel to meet the squad the following day. I texted him saying if there was anything he needed, he had only to ask. Watching the tackle again, I question whether it was a sending off. It was clumsy, sure – but Ramsey was far too quick for Ryan and that was that. With it being Stoke v Arsenal, of course, it was the perfect opportunity for everyone to make a big thing of it.

I have all the sympathy for Aaron but I have to say that I felt an awful accident – and that's what it was – was used to fuel the fire of some ill-placed vendetta. Stoke, as a club, were only interested in Aaron's welfare. Ryan and the club tried to make sure Aaron was alright but he wasn't interested – each to their own on that one – Aaron was more than entitled to do that. I just didn't like the reaction from others afterwards. Hounding someone who is going through distress of their own isn't really the greatest thing to do. My mind goes back to when Rory Delap was injured by Robbie Elliott – not one Stoke player hounded Robbie and got on his back. It was an accident.

There's a physical and psychological impact that players who suffer these serious injuries go through – I know that as well as anyone – but what about the damage to the reputation of the players who meant no malice?

Arsene Wenger said that Martin Taylor, the former Birmingham City defender whose tackle injured Eduardo in 2008, should never step foot on to a football pitch again. He said that if Ryan's tackle was part of football, then it wasn't a sport he wanted to be involved in.

It did knock Ryan's confidence for a bit but he did eventually recover. If he played for another club he may have had a stronger chance of playing more for his country, although England had better centre halves in Cahill and Jagielka. I'm sure Ryan wouldn't mind me saying that, just as he wouldn't mind me saying that versatility isn't quite a strength in getting him selected for the squad. I once saw him play at right back at Blackburn and he wasn't the most comfortable, let's say it that way. That said, he should still have more caps. Perhaps that incident had a negative effect on his international career immediately afterwards.

People who know Ryan know he's a lovely lad without an ounce of malice in him; the only people who think otherwise are people who simply don't know him at all.

Jumping ahead, when I do radio interviews in my current media role, Arsenal fans still bring up the Ramsey incident five or more years down the line.

When I'm asked how I think Arsenal will do, I give my honest answer. In one of these interviews, in Autumn 2013, I mentioned the handshaking incident, and when I got home I had loads of tweets from annoyed Arsenal fans saying what did I expect after the Ramsey incident. It goes to show just how angry and irrational it has made some people.

Fortunately, we're talking about two players who managed to get over that incident and progress. We all need to move on now so that every time Arsenal play Stoke, it's no longer mentioned. Let's congratulate Aaron Ramsey for coming back an even better player – what incredible mental toughness. I'm not just blaming Arsenal fans; Stoke fans bring it up, too. I'm just saying, move on, enough time has passed. Let's talk about Stoke evolving, and Arsenal's fantastic football.

The entire mood around the club was sombre following the injury to Aaron. A lot of Stoke players were affected by it. Tony advised us all to be extra careful with our media work, in case our words got twisted.

In general, we managed to deal with the negative publicity or the perception of how physical our play was pretty well but then there were the odd events – exceptions to the rule that people used as examples to suggest they were the norm. Eventually we got back to the normal atmosphere around the club at just around the right time.

A convincing win over Hull put us in 10th place with six games left. We were 15 points clear of relegation – there was little to no chance of us being dragged into it. Even with that in mind, when we travelled to Chelsea and were on the wrong end of a hiding, it was unacceptable. We were 3-0 down at half-time and there was an inquisition in the changing room; it was embarrassing, and it didn't get any better in the second half, with an atrocious 45 minutes which saw us concede another four goals.

In the week between the Chelsea game and our next, our last home game of the season against Everton, a lot of home truths were said. We didn't need telling more than once, we were good at looking in the mirror and accepting responsibility and we made up for it with a scoreless draw.

When we won 1-0 at Fulham in our penultimate game of the season, we recorded our 14th clean sheet in the Premier League, which was a very proud record.

On the last day, we played United at Old Trafford. Most of us were already on our holidays, mentally. I scored an own goal in a 4-0 defeat at the Stretford End. I'd dreamed of scoring at the Stretford End but not in those circumstances!

There was never a danger of us suffering from second season syndrome in the end. We finished a position higher, had a better points tally, had set a club record and had secured safety a lot earlier than we did the previous year.

It was a year to be proud at Stoke and it's a points tally for the club that Tony never matched; it was a further vindication of his management style that we improved in that second year. It perhaps got a little more difficult to maintain as time went on and we became more established but he was still able to effectively work his underdog routine. In public he'd play up the opposition, whoever they were, giving them credit and labelling them as favourites while in the dressing room he'd be telling us we were definitely capable of beating our opponents.

He was simplifying things and making me a far better player than I would have been in any other Premier League team. If it sounds like I'm romanticising a team that was brutal in others' eyes then look at my record for the first two seasons in the Premier League with Stoke – I had one booking, which I picked up ironically enough in that first game against Arsenal where van Persie had been sent off. Just one yellow from two years of playing against top players – and although some might question my ability, (and plenty have!) – they couldn't say I was a shirker who dodged tackles.

I went into everything and put my head in places people wouldn't put their feet. No-one ever said I needed to get stuck in more, let's put it that way. I'd like to say that my honesty helped but honesty never stopped you mistiming a tackle.

The only time I ever really saw the red mist – on the pitch – was in that incident with Steed Malbranque. I was as uncompromising as the team I was representing but hopefully as fair as my disciplinary record seemed to suggest.

Following my recall to the team in January, Mark O'Connor, one of our coaches, spoke to the media saying that my attitude was 'terrific' and that I'd been one of the better players. At the age of 31, I was confident that the best was still to come from both me and the club.

17

As Good As
It Gets

I had spent time in the Premier League with Derby County and Southampton but after such a fantastic time with Stoke City it might be fair to say that heading into the 2010/11 season, with two full seasons at that level with the Potters behind me, I finally felt like I'd become a recognised Premier League player.

We really established ourselves in that second year and had proven our style wasn't a flash in the pan. It was difficult for teams to contend with and it was for that reason that there was a good deal of optimism going into the new campaign.

Tony made some smart signings that summer, as he usually did. He would still ask my advice – although when we signed

James Beattie, he actually asked me what I thought, and then told me in the same conversation he'd already signed him! But instances like that only really helped to strengthen the bond between us.

We signed Carlo Nash that summer. He was very much a reserve goalkeeper and wasn't called upon very often but was a great lad to have around the place. In August, we signed Kenwyne Jones, who I'd obviously played with before, and was the kind of player that Tony liked. Jon Walters, too, was a great lad. Then, on deadline day, we signed Eidur Gudjohnsen – a very good footballer who just didn't seem to be a 'Stoke' player. Technically gifted, but he didn't suit the system we often used. Tuncay and Dave Kitson were in a similar bracket. Kits, for me, was the best of the three at adapting to what we needed, in terms of chasing down balls and so on, but even his strengths were not best utilised in the way we set up.

Could it be said that Tony was trying to change the way we played? I'm not sure. It wasn't broke, so he had no need to try and fix it. However, it's fair to say that there was an increased expectancy which meant we all had to up our game.

I didn't have a particularly great game in our opener to the season, against Wolves, and I was dropped as a result. On the Monday after the game we had a team meeting to speak about the loss and it all seemed to be about the mistakes I'd made. I'm the first to admit I played poorly but I felt Tony went over the top.

My next game was against Fulham in the League Cup, and I did quite well, scoring too. I felt I'd done enough to give myself a chance against Newcastle on the Saturday but I was back on the bench. We won, and Danny Collins had a great game, so I had little argument. It was an injury to Danny that saw me reach a landmark – he suffered a bad gash to his knee against Manchester United, so I came on for what was my 200th Premier League appearance. I wasn't one to look back and far from being satisfied with the achievement, I was upset that I hadn't been playing. Looking at it now, yeah, it's a record I'm proud of, but I was hoping to have had more at the time. I didn't think that giving me a game here or there would be getting the best out of me; I needed to be playing often, you couldn't put me in at 70 per cent and expect me to be at my best. I just wanted to look forward, I felt that the second I looked back was the second it all might end.

Being in that mindset meant I was never a big shirt swapper. I would also never swap my shirt if we'd had a hiding and unfortunately, I've been on the wrong end of a few – which means I've probably lost out on some good shirts! I just find it disrespectful to my team-mates and supporters. If I've had a stinker or we've suffered a demoralising defeat I would hardly be in the mood to chase a player for a souvenir of the occasion. I'm reminded of Andre Santos chasing Robin van Persie at half-time – half-time! – between Man Utd and Arsenal. What an embarrassment. Each to their own at full time but doing it on your way to the tunnel is not the way to do it.

I have, of course, swapped some shirts when the time was appropriate to do so. I'm a United fan and my shirts with players there include Jonny Evans, a lad I spent some time with at Sunderland, and also Paul Scholes. I was fortunate enough that if I ever did swap shirts with a player, more often than not I'd get the chance to play against them again, so in the next match I'd take the shirt along and get the kitman or someone to try and make sure the shirt got signed at the end of the game. It's for my son, Jak, to have a few shirts when he grows up.

They call it shirt 'swapping' but I never really thought anyone would want mine. After I asked Paul for his, I was walking off the pitch, and I heard Scholesy shouting me. "You better give me your shirt as well!"

That summed that generation up, really – what he was going to do with my shirt, I don't know. I guarantee it won't be framed and hung up in his house but to be asked was a very respectful gesture. In the Champions League final of 2011, even the likes of Xavi and Andres Iniesta were chasing Scholesy to get his shirt, which tells you everything you need to know. I felt very privileged.

Scholes was a genius and although at Stoke we had a small pitch, he made it look like the biggest in the league such was his ability to spread the play. He was one of the reasons why they had so much joy when they came to the Britannia.

Since I've retired, I've had a chance to go through all my shirts and choose some I want framed.

It was ironic, in a way, that after not featuring so often at the start of the season, I was rewarded with a new contract in the week following our defeat to United.

Tony looked after the players that he liked and I'd approached him earlier in the season saying I was thinking of leaving because I wanted to play regular football. His response was to say I had over 18 months left on my deal, and he wanted to give me a new contract because of everything that I'd done for the club and because he wanted to keep me around.

If it was based on my performances, I'm sure there's no way

I'd have been getting a new deal, but because I was a 'leader' in the dressing room, Tony felt he should reward me. I ummed and ahhed about it and spoke to my agent, Alex, who said I should sign the contract because it at least gave me the security of a longer deal. This turned out to be great advice.

Regardless of whether I had one or five years on my contract, I wanted to be playing. I did get minutes, but I was in and out of the team and it wasn't ideal. I played well in our FA Cup game against Cardiff City, which we drew. With about three minutes to go, I went on an overlap but pulled my hamstring. I came off for Rory, and learned I had a grade one/two strain which meant I'd probably be out for two or three weeks. It was frustrating, considering I'd just got back in the team. I was training but I knew, realistically, that I wasn't right – I could only really run at about two thirds of my normal pace.

On Friday morning, Dave Watson came up and said that he'd heard if I was fit, I'd be playing against Bolton. I said that was fine – I was – but Dave questioned it as he knew I'd not been right. We had a couple of fitness tests and the gaffer said he'd play me but I didn't have to train, I just had to watch the set-pieces. I played, and scored, against Bolton, but after the game I told Dave to make sure I wasn't selected against Cardiff in the replay.

Next thing I hear the squad's been announced, I'm not only travelling but I'm playing and captain. I try and tell the gaffer but he says, "Don't worry, if anything happens I'll take responsibility." He persuaded me, but surprise surprise, within three or four minutes my hamstring went and I had to come off.

I was out for a few weeks – my return was at Liverpool in early February, as we lost to a Luis Suarez goal on his debut.

Suarez had obviously just joined them following the departure of Fernando Torres, who went to Chelsea for a British record fee of £50m. Torres is a player I've always liked to see do well – apart from against me – because he's such a hard worker but looking at his career since I think anyone would say that Liverpool did good business at the time. I felt I'd done okay again against Liverpool but when it came to preparing for our next game, against Birmingham, Tony was setting up his team and it was clear he was preferring Danny Pugh, a left-sided midfielder, at left back – that felt like a bit of a kick in the teeth. Not that it was Danny, just that he was out of position. To be fair to him, even though we lost the Birmingham game, he played quite well.

I was jumping on to a rollercoaster of emotions that was to last a few weeks. We went to West Ham when my wife was due to give birth. I went to see the manager and explained the situation, asking if it was okay if I missed the game because I hadn't really been playing as of late. Tony said it was alright and I was grateful for that. West Ham beat us 3-0 in March to put us in a precarious position, as my son Joshua was born.

It was a tough defeat to take as even though we were in 12th position, there were only four points separating us from the relegation zone with nine games left and West Ham, in 17th place, had closed the gap on us. The Hammers were our next opponents, too, in the FA Cup quarter-final.

Of the many great things I've got to say about Tony Pulis, another is that when times are hard, he goes back to people he can trust, and that meant that I was going to be back in the team for this very important game.

I was optimistic and feeling good, mainly because of the birth of Joshua, but I was also spurred on by the fact that a lot of my best football had come in the wake of my children being born. I think that was simply because when I'd had struggles previously, I'd only had football to concentrate on, but having kids gives you a different perspective. It's a gentle reminder that there are more important things in life. Having something to take your mind off the game can ironically help you focus on it.

Playing in the quarter-final represented the opportunity to get to Wembley, something I'd never yet done. For six seasons, between 2000 and 2006, of course, the Millennium Stadium had been used for the FA Cup. If I could be part of the team that got us there, I felt Tony would keep faith with that team.

It was a tight affair. We scored early on through Huth, but then Piquionne equalised. Then we were awarded a penalty in the first few seconds of the second half – Matty Etherington won it when he drove forward at a defender and committed him into a challenge.

In my absence, James Beattie had taken penalties, and with me not being in the team as regularly since James had left, Matty took them. He took this one and Rob Green pulled off a great save.

Instead of feeling deflated, we kept up the pressure and won a free-kick just outside the box. I thought about trying to get the kick but it was probably just a little too far out for me. Jermaine Pennant took it instead and his attempt was handled by Carlton Cole, so another free-kick a bit closer was awarded.

As it was so close, it put off those who wanted the space to be able to get the ball over the wall and back down again. Instead, Robert Huth and Ryan Shawcross would stand in the middle of the wall and allow a strike through them.

This was my opportunity.

I took the kick and smashed it – it took the slightest nick off Scott Parker, though the power would make it difficult for Rob Green anyway.

He got a hand to it and knocked it on to the post but couldn't stop it going in, and my first reaction was to look over at the linesman.

Has he given it?

Does he think Green stopped it before it crossed the line?

For me, the wait seemed to last a lifetime – then he took one step towards the halfway line and ran back.

Defending is great but scoring a goal, particularly one as important as that, is a feeling I cannot describe. I look back at the replays of my celebration and think, "Danny, what the fuck are you doing?!"

I wasn't a forward who netted 15 to 30 times a season and had a celebration planned. Yeah, I did well for a defender, but I'd never scored anything as significant as that and it was a sensational feeling. It sunk in then that we were close to Wembley… it was backs to the wall as West Ham poured forward but we defended manfully and the joy which greeted the final whistle was tangible.

The Britannia was euphoric.

We went back onto the pitch for a warm down and loads of supporters were still there – there was a special atmosphere around the ground and that continued through the week. One day, a lad came in with the ball that I'd apparently scored with and asked me to sign it. Everything was bubbling around the club. There was a lot of talk about it being our first semi-final for a very long time.

For our next league game, it was no surprise when Newcastle United came to town and we hammered them on a day everything seemed to go right. It was almost like a celebration, in spite of the trouble we'd had in the league.

In many ways, Tony's decision to start with a strong team in the FA Cup was two fingers up to those who choose to play weakened sides in the competition.

The argument for doing that is that it keeps players fresh, that playing your first choice in the cup will be detrimental to league form, but looking at how we responded to that West Ham game speaks volumes for the argument against. It had an invigorating effect – we won three and drew three of our seven games after the game against West Ham.

The win over Newcastle was one of the best performances I was involved in during my time at Stoke. We won 4-0 against a strong side – though Sol Campbell, near the end of his career, didn't have the greatest of games. We were already 2-0 up when I stepped up for a free-kick, slightly further back than the week before. I took a long run-up and absolutely smashed it into the net.

My celebration this time was a bit more measured but I was just as delighted – to score two good goals, two weeks running and now to be part of this great performance, with a clean sheet, made me think that there was no way this team would get relegated now.

The draw for the semi-final pitted four teams from the same area against each other – Manchester United and Manchester City, Bolton Wanderers and ourselves. I'm sure Bolton hoped the same, that they would get us, as it meant a better chance of getting to the final, and that was how it transpired.

The momentum was too strong. It had been a difficult season up to that point but what with the birth of another child and the goals – and the manner of them – it's hard for me to recollect a time in my career that I was doing as well as I was in the early spring of 2011.

18

Dear Diary

An international break followed the win over Newcastle – my wife's family came over and we had a really nice week. On the Saturday between games, we had a big get-together to wet the baby's head. I got steaming – I took the dog out for a walk and fell into a bush halfway down the street! On Monday I was back in training and preparing for the Chelsea game the next weekend.

Chelsea loved playing through the middle – their wingers would come inside and work their way through in that way. We had a training session on the Britannia the day before, and at the end of it we had a five-a-side right down the middle of the pitch. Tony's idea was to break the ground up where Chelsea liked to play.

The size of the pitch was great, and the wide areas were fine – which obviously suited our gameplan, too. On matchday it was clear to see that the pitch had been abused. It wasn't especially for Chelsea, this was something Tony would do for any of the passing teams – he'd let the grass grow long, too, to make it difficult for the ball to fly around. He'd deliberately not water the pitch as well – part of our gameplan was hitting the ball forward for flick-ons and Tony's horticultural interests played a significant part in that.

Against Chelsea, the ball was bobbling around all over the place, making it difficult for them to get into their usual rhythm. We took an early lead when Jon Walters scored a great goal. They equalised before half-time but we absolutely battered them in the second half, we just couldn't find that second goal that we deserved.

Whenever we've been on the verge of a big result before, Tony would always try and make sure we kept our composure in the final minutes, meaning no unnecessary risks; protect what we have, that kind of mentality. Even if we got a corner, we'd leave three back – and I'd always be one of those three. For some reason – probably, the momentum of how everything had been going – I went up for a corner we won. I didn't hear Tony yelling at me to get back so I thought I was okay, and I'll be honest, I fancied my chances of getting another goal.

The ball was played in and I went up for the header – Petr Cech went up with me and misjudged it. For a split second, I thought I was going to score again. I headed it and Branislav Ivanovic cleared it off the line.

Then I landed from my jump.

I came down on a straight leg and Cech's boot caught me just underneath my knee, on my calf. When I say he caught me, I mean, he barely touched me, there was hardly any contact at all but because I was on a straight leg, my knee buckled from what contact there was. It went one way then the other. I hopped up as if something had fallen on my foot but was back on the floor in no time.

Previously, I've broken my femur and had a disc pop in my back – but nothing came close to the pain I was feeling at that moment. I've seen the replays. I'm smashing the floor with my fist, kicking it with my other leg.

Chelsea played on. Torres went through and nearly scored. Cech came up to me and asked me if I was okay – Kenwyne was quick on the scene too. I couldn't reply to anyone, I couldn't speak, I was in so much pain.

Dave Watson and the Doc came on the pitch – I've always been straight up with any injuries I've felt, I've never tried to overplay them, and Dave realised that which is why he brought on the doctor too. They turned me over on my back, and messed around with my knee – all of a sudden, the pain was gone.

"Thank God for that" I think.

Must have been a dead leg.

Dave checked my cruciate. At first, he thought I'd dislocated my kneecap, but told me he could 'feel an end point'. Apparently if you can do that, the cruciate is intact. He did a few exercises and told me I'd got away with it – little did I know at the time, but my leg had just gone into spasm.

When I stood up I said I felt like a bit of a prick. I said I felt silly – all that pain and then it was just gone. I ran back to the halfway line. I was waved back on as we attacked, and the ball went out for a goal kick.

Cech took the kick and I was straight in to an aerial challenge with Didier Drogba.

I jumped off the right leg, the one I'd just hurt, and as I was landing, my leg was just swinging in the air.

It looked, and felt, odd.

The ball went out of play and I just sat on the floor. The lads asked me what I was doing – but I couldn't move properly. Chelsea players were surrounding me saying "Get off the fucking pitch!" No chance – we'd be down to ten, a defender light, right at the end of the game.

The referee came over and I told him I just couldn't move. Dave came on again and this time I was helped off. The substitution was made. I was given a warm reception by the crowd – which included my father-in-law, watching me play live for the first time (he considered himself an unlucky omen after that, as you might imagine). I headed into the dressing room.

Dave said he could still feel the end point – we discussed the game coming up against Tottenham the following week, and even though I left the ground on crutches, I was still optimistic I would be alright. It was just a precaution.

That evening, Scouse came over. I asked him to have a look at my knee and he said that he wasn't that convinced by it. To him, it felt all over the place. He said the only thing in my favour was that it wasn't swollen, and without that, he couldn't be sure whether I'd done my cruciate or not.

I had a tubular grip on it to keep the swelling down but as I got into bed, it was starting to hurt, so I just ripped it off. I woke up at eight the next morning and it looked like someone had injected my knee with about five litres of water. It had completely blown up.

I got in my car and drove to the ground – when I saw Dave, I told him to just tell me the truth, no buttering it up.

"You've done your cruciate."

"Fucking hell Dave, I wanted you to be honest but I hoped you might say something else!"

I asked him what the next stage was and he started talking about scans but then it hit me…

Wembley.

I'd never played there before and now I was going to miss my chance. I'd miss the final if we got there too. I was pissed off for the rest of the day. Not exactly feeling sorry for myself, but I was 32, I'd worked hard and had a decent career, I was in great form and I felt that playing at Wembley would really be the cherry on the icing. That month summed up life in general. You have to take the rough with the smooth and have to find a silver lining. I believe most things happen for a reason. Talking to my wife later that day, I just couldn't rationalise it.

The lowest point was the day after, Monday, when we had to do a shoot for ESPN, who were covering the semi-final. We had to wear our kits and have our photos taken – I talked to the gaffer and asked him if I could miss it. I was on crutches, was having a scan that afternoon and was almost certainly out for the foreseeable. Why did I need to be there? Tony said it was part of the contract. One of the lads had to help me put my shorts and socks on, and when we got out into the stadium, the photographers were telling me where to walk and where to stand. It felt like adding insult to injury, literally.

The lads went off for a day trip to Wembley to have a look around. Meanwhile, I headed off for my scan. I'd established a good relationship with the guy who did my scans and he would normally give me a pretty good idea of what was wrong with me before the results came back.

He'd say, "Don't take it as gospel, but…" and he was always spot on. I went in for the scan and asked him what was wrong.

"Danny, normally I give you a hunch, but this isn't a hunch, it's 100 per cent certain. If I didn't know better I'd think you'd been in a skiing accident. Your cruciate is completely snapped."

I went back to the training ground – Dave had gone with the lads to Wembley but got the email through confirming the scan results. I started to get a lot of texts from the lads sending their best wishes. Rory, who'd missed the cup final at Southampton, got in touch. I tried to keep a brave face on it – I reasoned that Rory finally had his chance to play at Wembley and hopefully I would get some opportunity in the future too.

I'm not ashamed to admit that when I got home I cried my eyes out. 'Cruciate' is still probably the worst word you can say to a footballer and it couldn't have come at a worse time for me.

I couldn't accept it. I went into the club a couple of days later and asked the doctor if he could give me injections that would get me through the semi-final. He looked at me as if I was daft. He said I had to see the bigger picture – I repeated my wish but he said there wasn't, and even if there was, he wouldn't give it me. Then I went to see Roger Oldham in Leicester – apparently he had been able to help some people in similar situations before.

My issue was that my cruciate was completely torn – if there was a slight connection between one side and the other, he might be able to try and sort something. If it had worked, it wouldn't have got me right for the semi-final, but I was hoping it might get me right for the final if we got there.

It was a waste of time.

Fair play to him for trying, though.

I saw the surgeon and he said I was very fortunate – I'd injured my medial and my knee, but there were no complications. Once my medial had healed he said he would operate, and I was having injections and going to the gym every day to strengthen my knee, so it was strong enough to have an operation. It was hard to do, as the way I was seeing it was that I was strengthening it up for it to be ripped to pieces.

For a while, I didn't want to have anything to do with football or Stoke City. The buzz around the club was the semi-final and I just didn't want any part of it. I'd go in when I knew the lads were finishing training. I wasn't being selfish – well, I'd like to think so, but there was probably an element of that – but I didn't feel as if I was a part of it so I just didn't want to know. I began to write a diary and I suppose now, when I'm putting this story of my career and life so far together, it seems a good time to share some extracts from it. The diary started with my thoughts in the hours after I suffered my injury.

> **Saturday, April 2nd, 2011:** *Be strong, everything happens for a reason. Look at it as a challenge to overcome and resurrect my career. That career is not over. I will show all the doubters and play in the Premiership again… shit happens and if you recover properly the rewards will feel that much better!*

It wasn't long before the semi-final against Bolton, which took place on Sunday, April 17th. I was driven down to the game and was dropped outside Wembley – the taxi could only get so far, but fortunately enough, where I had to enter was at the Stoke end.

As I walked into the stadium, thousands of Stoke fans were chanting my name and clapping – it was a really touching moment. Seeing banners that said, "Do it for Danny," meant so much.

I went in to see the lads but the feeling of not wanting to be there returned. The boss said I could be a great help, just being around, but that wasn't the point – I didn't want to, and I know that looks like an awful thing to say, but it was just how I felt. I was delighted that they won and won so convincingly on the day – 5-0 in front of more than 75,000 fans – and afterwards, the lads were coming up and saying that the win was for me.

I couldn't wait to get away.

Monday, April 18th: Missing not one but two trips to Wembley is something that's been on my mind but I have to get my head around it ASAP. It's so frustrating… I do have the odd occasion where I think 'why me?' but I'm trying to quickly get out of that by counting my blessings. I'm very fortunate. It's a trying time.

Tuesday, April 26th: Tomorrow is the day of the operation and I just want to get it done. I went to the ground this evening to see the lads before they beat Wolves 3-0. It was good to see them but I couldn't wait to get away from there and left before kick-off. They were all nice, the staff were too, wishing me all the best… obviously it's not like I can't stand the place. Far from it. It's just the feeling that I can't do what I have always done all my life and I miss that feeling I get when I go on to the pitch or training ground. I think I was starting to take it for granted, but it's true, that feeling when you get back into the dressing room after a game where you've just performed well... that few minutes, it's a hard feeling to beat.

Saturday, April 30th: Had the operation three days ago and everything went well – I'm home now. The surgeon said the rest of my knee is in good shape which is good to hear after 16 years of professional football. I knew that after the operation I'd be a bit down but today is definitely my lowest point as far as emotions and anger are concerned. I feel tired, snappy, in pain and even walking to the toilet feels almost like an impossible task. Honestly, at this moment in time, I wish I hadn't had the operation because of the pain and stress it's caused. Hopefully the next few days will change that...

Wednesday, May 4th: It's 1am early Wednesday morning. Because I can't sleep I may as well catch up on my diary. The main reasons I can't sleep are due to giving up on my sleeping pills which I needed to do and also the pain in my knee, which has been getting worse the last couple of days. I really thought after the first few days of the op any little pains I had would be gone but I can honestly say the last *few days the pain has been excruciating, especially when my leg has been up straight then I get up to walk. It feels like my knee and front of my shin are on fire and are going to explode and I know I will change my feelings but at this point there is a large percentage of me feeling I should not have had the operation and just called it a day with football, which is quite a sobering feeling but just how I feel at this moment. I feel useless. Nicole is having to take care of two babies – Joshua, and me. She really is an angel. Without her this would have been overwhelming. I don't like having to rely on anybody. I hate not being able to pick up my boy out of his cot when he is crying.*

I got a bit worried the evening of this diary entry. The pain and pressure in my shin and knee was getting worse, to the point where I was struggling to hide it from the kids, so I called Dave and he told me it was normal. I wasn't convinced.

We went out for dinner and just as we sat down I couldn't believe my eyes, Dai Rees came in. He came straight over to ask how I was feeling, so I explained about the pain. He took a look at it and said it looked good… he said because of the operation I'd had, using patella tendon instead of the hamstring, it would be more painful at first, but it would then be stronger in the long run, so that put my mind at rest completely.

He also told me I had to realise I had major surgery and that it was a long recovery so I shouldn't expect to feel great straight away. Maybe he was right. I felt like I hadn't got my head completely around what had happened.

My aim was to come back fitter and physically and mentally stronger than I was before my injury. If I could do that, then I knew everything would be okay.

It was up to me...

Friday, May 6th: Having a good day today. I feel like I have turned a bit of a very small corner with the pain starting to subside but I know I have a long road ahead. Today I was able to get on a bike. It took me a while to turn the pedals because of the stiffness of my knee but I eventually got there. I turned it ten times and got off and can honestly say I felt like I had just played 90 minutes of a hard game. I knew I would have to start somewhere, it just seemed a pretty low starting point. I do feel I was taking it for granted. I used to moan if training was shit or we didn't do enough. I can safely say that will not be happening again. When I get back on the pitch, I will savour every moment, running included.

As the cup final approached, I still felt disconnected from the club. The only shining light for me was that my injury meant that Andy Wilkinson would get a chance and he was Stoke through and through. If anyone deserved to play in my absence it was him.

Saturday, May 14th: FA Cup final day. Feeling very low and uninterested in what is a historic day. I feel I should be playing... everybody was telling me they felt for me and that I got them to the semi-

final with my goal, but for me, unless you're actually playing the game you have no right to feel involved. I feel like I'm in a bit of a dark place again, still seven months of rehab away from kicking a ball. Half of me feels like retiring while the other half is telling me to get a grip and grow the fuck up. I know by writing my thoughts down every day it will help along the way...

It was hard to get through cup final day knowing I should have been a part of it. I was reminded of a comparison with Roy Keane and Paul Scholes in the Champions League final of 1999 but at least they played a huge part in the semi-final. They deserved to celebrate with the team after the final because they were the reason they got there, or a massive part of it, whereas I just felt like I'd helped us get to the last four.

I suppose I had more right to feel involved than I did when I was at Southampton but the simple fact of the matter was that I didn't.

I felt for Ricardo, who missed the final too. He was a massive part of Stoke's history. Like me, he put on a brave face. I simply didn't want to be there.

The club got me a medal – that was nice, but it means little to me. It's not my achievement, it's just something that was given to me. At Southampton I had at least 'earned' my loser's medal by being named in the squad. I hadn't done that with Stoke.

There are similarities between the two finals, I suppose.

Stoke played very well on the day but Manchester City scored late on and you would have to say that they deserved to win the game. There's no point romanticising it and saying anything else. Stoke had at least qualified for Europe by getting to the final as City were in the Champions League. That was a truly historic achievement.

Monday, May 16th: *Got a lot of mixed feelings today. Firstly, the cup final is out of the way… as bad as it sounds, we lost, and a small part of me was quite happy. It's an awful thing to feel and not one I like having to feel. I love the lads, and I love the club, but I couldn't have been able bear seeing them celebrating without me being a part of it. It really is awful to feel and I'm not proud of myself but that's the truth. It's so selfish. Now it's gone, it feels like a big burden is off my shoulders. I don't have to feel like I'm missing anything. It's Nicole and mine's first wedding anniversary tomorrow and if someone had said that within that year we'd have a son and I'd have a messed-up knee I'd have thought they were crazy.*

Monday, July 11th: *The club went to Austria for pre-season but they've allowed me to stay at home which is great. It's just a lonely day starting at 8.30am and finishing at 3.30pm. I do feel a bit low; although I'm jogging on a trampoline, and in the pool, I know that I'm missing out on the pre-season. Three to five hours in the gym every day to try and get muscle back in my leg and get my knee moving. It's very painful with little reward. At times over the last few days during my circuit I have felt like giving up…*

I just have to keep going. Hopefully in three or four weeks I'll be able to jog in a straight line. And five or six weeks after that, hopefully twisting and turning. It's one hell of a grind but the thought of putting my boots on again for a game of football at any level is keeping me going.

Friday, September 23rd: *Well, I'm counting down the days until I am back training and hopefully that will be in ten days if everything keeps progressing. Touch wood, I haven't had too many setbacks over the last six months. Dave has been fantastic helping me with my rehab. I owe you one, Dave. You've been brilliant. The end is in sight – training on October 3rd, and a reserve game against Sheffield United on October 11th. If I'm training well then maybe the Europa League game against Maccabi Tel Aviv on the 20th. Nicole (and my friends and family) have been crucially important in my recovery. I am truly blessed.*

Cruciate injuries have ruined and ended careers and as the days went by, my only thoughts were on getting back fit to play football. Playing for Stoke City was a secondary issue; playing in the Premier League, too, was an afterthought.

What represented success for me was getting past the injury and just playing professional football again.

19

End Of An Era

When I was young, my parents worked tirelessly to provide for us. I would always remember Dad saying "Do you want better than this?" and that served as my motivation. If I wanted a better lifestyle, I had the opportunity, however slim, to make a career from football. For better or worse, I wasn't the best academically, my parents knew that and concentrated their efforts on making sure I had everything in place. They never told me to not concentrate on schoolwork, but they made sure that if I ever needed anything – right down to those black strap molasses – I'd get it.

Fast forward a few years and my son, Jak, is a keen footballer. The difference between him and me is that I've been fortunate enough to succeed and provide him with that lifestyle that

I've worked hard for. I can't turn around to him and ask if he wants to 'better' what he has because he wants for nothing at the present time. He's a lot brighter than I was, so I stress on him the importance of his education.

I was obviously at United when I sat my GCSEs but because I was training I wasn't able to collect my results, so we got them sent to our homes. When results morning came around we all called our parents. My mum answered to tell me I'd got four D's, two E's and a G. I came off the phone and told the lads. I found it funny at the time. It was probably just the innocence of youth but looking back, I just think I completely got away with it. I was lucky. It wasn't a laughing matter. I've always said that if Jak's education begins to suffer because of his football commitments then there is only one winner, and it isn't football.

When he was eight he got offered a contract to go to Crewe Alexandra. A contract! This is nothing against Crewe, it's the way things work now.

My best times growing up playing football were playing for Sunday teams like Stretford Vics. I remember winning a national five-a-side competition where the prize was to watch England play Cameroon at Wembley. It was brilliant.

All those kind of enjoyments have been taken away with the way academies are. I said to Jak that I didn't want him to sign the contract. He could go to Crewe, just not on a contract. I thought he didn't need the pressure, but then he got upset and started crying so I relented. I told him he had to understand it's a 100 per cent commitment – too much for a kid I thought. Tuesday and Thursday training, half five until eight, optional training on a Friday and a game on Sunday. He stuck at it but when he got to the age of 11, they released him.

To be fair to the club, they were probably right to, but in defence of Jak, he has a late July birthday so in reality he should have been playing for the year below as physically he wasn't developed as much as the other boys. He was upset, naturally, but I said it was the best thing for him – it enabled him to have a more relaxed childhood, it freed him to play Sunday football again with his mates. We sorted him out with the local team in Betley and he loved it.

Recently he got in touch with me to say Port Vale wanted him to go down there – he started training, and then sent me a text to tell me he'd played for them and did really well, hitting the bar. He said that he'd taken Crewe for granted – maybe so, but he's just a kid. The environment isn't great – I'd go and watch him play and you'd hear all the parents saying "this or that team want my son" – I had to take a step away from it. There's enough pressure on the kids anyway but most of it comes from the parents. It's not fair on them, and I've seen many drop away at the age of 14 or 15 because they've had enough. It's wrong and takes the enjoyment away.

What was wrong with the old system? Centre of excellence and the ability to play Sunday League with your mates. You now have kids who might go to a club at eight and get released at 16 – they've spent eight years – half their life! – with their sole and principle aim to become a footballer. All the sacrifices they've made and they get thrown on the scrapheap.

Don't get me wrong, I made those sacrifices too, but at least I had a childhood. You're robbing kids of theirs these days. Clubs have their own systems too and that means that all the natural talent, all that natural ability that once made them stand out all too often gets coached out of them.

Kids need things simplifying, they need to be able to express themselves. You don't want robots.

A few years ago I knew a bloke, Jeff, his son was called Frazer and was a goalkeeper at Crewe. One day I bumped into Jeff at the club and asked how things were – he said that Frazer had just been released, so I asked if I could go and have a word with him. I went to the car and this ten-year-old lad is sat crying his eyes out. I felt so much for him – I told him not to worry about it and just enjoy his football. Imagine turning around to a kid of that age and telling them they're not good enough?

It's nothing to do with my Stoke connections but my hope is that my son just enjoys his football rather than committing himself to Port Vale, or anyone for that matter. I'll always do my best to give him what he wants but let's just say my thoughts on it are very clear! It's a pressurised industry, so of course it comes with the territory but there has to be a better way. There once was, after all. I have to stress it's not about the academies or the clubs, it's just the rules they have to follow.

I had plenty of time to form football opinions during my rehab. I was now 32 and I was conscious about my body and whether or not I would be the same player when I got back. If I got back. There was no guarantee. It was almost a point to prove by itself, to show everyone that I could make a return.

At my age I think it could have been easy to retire or not be as dedicated. I had the security of two years still on my Stoke contract but that didn't even cross my mind. I think the most important thing for me was simply that I wanted to have that control; I wanted to be the one that decided when my career was over, and I wasn't ready for it to be over just yet.

When I broke my femur I'd cycle from Altrincham to the Cliff every day and that's a hell of a distance – I was that dedicated because I just loved the game. Now, my connection with the game had diminished.

It hadn't disappeared but I had a young family to think about, other things that consumed my time, and to be honest, the timing of the injury and having to be a part of these big events when I was injured had taken its toll a little bit.

The reality was that the injury had triggered the end of my career at Stoke City. The spell out with my femur worked to my advantage because I built up my other leg; there was no advantage to spending six months out at the age of 32. Stoke would move on as they obviously should, and then plan for their future accordingly. I was past my peak anyway, I had nothing really to prove to anyone and I was never going to come back physically better. Don't get me wrong – I was as dedicated to my recovery as I had been when I was younger, but the motivation was completely different.

I was managing that personal change and 'managing change' and different expectations was very much the theme at Stoke City, too, after three years of incredible success. What had worked so well with Tony was that he had always created that underdog spirit. That's what worked well for us. He'd managed that, to an extent, against anyone we came up against.

Even if it was a team we'd be expected to beat, Tony would build up the opposition in the press. Behind closed doors, like I said, he'd be talking much differently. After three years of life in the Premier League, though, he'd be fooling nobody if he said we were underdogs for every game. That would be an insult to the good work we'd put in, after all.

I suppose Stoke were becoming victims of their own success. If we'd finished 17th, 16th, 15th, the expectation would be easier to handle. But we'd finished mid-table and now played in an FA Cup final and qualified for Europe. In the period it took me to return from injury I have to admit that even though Tony still had time for me, it felt like the club had moved on. Top ten, a good run in the cup and a European experience were expected rather than hoped for.

Qualifying for Europe is a big achievement but the Europa League is a joke in my opinion. I can't see why they changed it from the UEFA Cup format, or the Cup Winners' Cup. People say it was changed because people lost interest, but people lost interest because of the changes to it. Playing on a Thursday and expecting players to play at the weekend is ridiculous.

I've no doubt in my mind Stoke's form suffered for their involvement and although there was a genuine intention to compete, it was very much a case that it shouldn't be at the expense of league points. The squad wasn't big enough to cope with it. Nobody really takes it seriously until the knockout rounds anyway. It's a shame because every competition should have an element of prestige.

There was never any expectation on Stoke to win the Europa League and they did well to reach the last 32, going out to Valencia in February, 2012, with narrow 1-0 defeats in both legs.

There was never really any danger of Tony's job being in danger if he failed to scale the heights he'd done previously at the club and that was refreshing to see. Given Stoke's historical average position, Tony was caught between a rock and a hard place in that he'd probably taken the club as far as could be expected. I have plenty of sympathy with managers not getting time, and it annoys me to see promoted teams getting rid of their manager part of the way into the season. Against that, you could argue that Crystal Palace looked in severe danger in 2013/14 until Tony took over from Ian Holloway.

One of my first games back was in the Europa League in Israel against Maccabi Tel Aviv and we won 2-0. I'd played a couple of reserve games – the BBC covered some of my comeback and I scored a free-kick in one of those games.

It was great to get on the pitch again but the fragility of our careers and our bodies after injury was brought home to me in one of those reserve games. I had shared some of my own rehab with Mama Sidibe, and in a game at Port Vale he got the slightest knock on the back of his knee – when I went over to him I couldn't see his kneecap. He'd dislocated and broken it – I was crestfallen for him, not just because I knew how he felt but because he's such a genuinely great guy who's suffered terribly with injuries. It was difficult to see.

I was grateful to be back but that incident really made me see things differently. I knew in my heart that I wasn't the same player – my body felt different. I'd lost a yard, I was running differently too.

The game in Israel suited me fine as the pace of the game was slower and I played in a back three; it was a good adjustment to get me back.

I was stiff the next day and on the Sunday we played Bolton. We got battered 5-0, revenge for the semi-final, though like I say that probably had far more to do with the scheduling. I came on for the last 15 minutes – it was nice to be on the pitch, even if I was breathing out of my arse at the end.

As he usually did, Tony made changes for the next game, and went back to his trusted servants after the disappointing defeat to Bolton. That included me – but looking back, I should never have played. I wasn't ready for a full game, even if I felt that I was at the time. I ran with a limp – I was embarrassing against QPR as we lost 3-2. Jamie Mackie ran me ragged. From me doing my cruciate to being back in the Premier League was about five and a half months. It was ridiculously soon and I should have known better. Maybe Tony should have, too – that game felt like it was the end of my Stoke career and that was a shame, for me. People have said I was thrown under the bus but I was as responsible as anyone.

I played against Dynamo Kiev and then at Besiktas in Europe. We'd already qualified for the next round – it was an amazing experience to see the passion of the Turkish supporters but even though we went ahead we were like rabbits in headlights, a bunch of lads not used to playing often, and we lost 3-1. That was the last time I played for the club even though the reality was that I was finished the second I did my cruciate. There are no grudges, no bitterness.

The injury had fast forwarded the inevitable by about a year but I had to face facts – if I wanted to continue to play football, and I did, I would have to find a new club.

I had more or less the entire Christmas of 2011 off. I wasn't included in the Stoke squads and I knew I'd be looking at a move in the January transfer window. I was getting offers from clubs that were miles away to go on loan – they were saying that I could train with Stoke and just turn up on a Friday. If I was going to go on loan I wanted to treat it like a proper move and be amongst the lads but I was at an age and time in life where I didn't want to be miles away from my family.

On deadline day, Nottingham Forest came in for me. The manager Steve Cotterill said he wanted me to make sure they stayed up. I decided to go and my first game was going be at my old club Derby. I was in a hotel in Nottingham, watching the news when it came on that Nigel Doughty, the owner of the club, had sadly passed away. The game wasn't called off for that reason, it was called off because of bad weather – but it was a very sombre atmosphere around the club considering all that Nigel had done and how highly regarded he was among the supporters and the players.

My first game was against Watford and we drew 1-1. Next, we lost at Middlesbrough, then won a hotly contested game against Coventry City. We went to Birmingham and won 2-1 but ten minutes in, my hamstring went and I had to come off – simply a consequence of too much football in a short space of time after so long without it.

I came back against Millwall and scored in a 3-1 win – I hurt my hamstring again, and though I finished the game, I was out for a while. I was hoping to get another chance in the team and thought I might get back in after Forest lost the re-arranged game at Derby, but Steve said he wasn't going to change the team. When I realised I wasn't part of Steve's plans going forward, and Forest recorded an incredible 7-3 win at Leeds, I approached him the following week.

I said that I'd been there to help them stay up and I felt I'd done that. Now he was just playing the lads who had permanent contracts. I had no problem with that but it obviously meant there was no place for me.

Steve more or less agreed, saying that Forest couldn't afford to get me the following season so he had to see if any of the other lads could step up in my place. Fair enough. I said I'd go back to Stoke because it was pointless me being there – but I promised that if the shit hit the fan and Forest needed me because of injuries, I'd go back and play.

I trained with Stoke for the rest of the season and when it came to the summer I had a dilemma; I had a year left on my contract but wasn't going to force a move.

You have your ups and downs at football clubs and the summer of 2012 was a time when Tony and I didn't get on great. I'd been at the club for more or less seven years. When we went to Heathrow to get the plane to America for our pre-season tour, I discovered that my ticket was in economy class while the rest of the first team were in first class. Myself, Michael Tonge and a couple of others had been put in economy. Tony said he hadn't sorted the tickets so I went to see John Rudge – I said that if he wanted me to leave the club then were ways and means of telling me and this wasn't one.

I felt it was taking the piss, moving me away from the rest of the lads. It wasn't about being in first class or economy, it was the principle of travelling separately, and I said that either John sorted it or I was going home. They did sort it out but the bad feeling had set in. When we were due to come back, I discovered the return flight was still in economy class so I said that either the club changed it, or I'd get my own flight and bill the club. I think that my attitude pissed off the gaffer but I felt that I was being disrespected.

He pulled me to one side one day while we were out there and said Ipswich were interested in taking me on loan. I wasn't keen, but thought if I could fly back, I'd have the opportunity to sort out a move elsewhere. Overall it wasn't a great way for things to end – but even if the gaffer was pissed off with me at that time, our relationship has been more than solid and sound enough to withstand it. He's done more than enough good to justify my praise and respect.

The loan move didn't happen and I wasn't involved in the squad for the start of the 2012/13 season. Dave Kemp, Tony's assistant, pulled me to one side on the morning of the day we were due to play Swindon Town in the League Cup and he said that not only would I not be playing, I was to train with the kids and play with them at Morecambe. I was so far out of the picture and it just felt like I was unwanted.

I didn't want things to end badly at Stoke, and when Ipswich came in again to take me on loan, I was hesitant again as I felt I'd done all my travelling. But I did go in the end. Paul Jewell, who was the Ipswich manager at the time is someone I have a lot of time for. He had a decent squad but the lads weren't per-forming – my addition strengthened the backline and we got decent draws at Barnsley and Brighton.

It felt like our fortunes were changing but then we lost the next four – Paul was sacked. Paul had tried to change tack with the players and had started being nice instead of critical; some of the players seemed to take advantage of that, and took their foot off the gas. There was no way back for Paul and the club was in a bit of a mess.

Mick McCarthy – who tried to sign me at Wolves – was the new boss with Terry Connor his assistant. They were brilliant. In their first game, we won at Birmingham and kept a clean sheet. I stayed because my loan had been extended by Paul.

TC enquired about how long I was thinking of staying and things seemed to be going well – but a few days later, it all came crashing down as we lost 5-0 at Crystal Palace. I was awful and then two weeks later I had another stinker as we got battered 6-0 at Leicester.

We drew 1-1 at home to Peterborough but I was responsible for their goal. We were due to play Forest the Tuesday after, but Mick pulled me aside and said, "Danny, I'm taking you out of the team because for the last few games you've been shit. You've cost us a lot of goals recently."

He'd earned my respect instantly by not messing around. I agreed – if I'd have played against Forest I wouldn't have been on it. The lads won and I was kept on the bench until my spell there was over. TC talked to me about coaching; he said I'd be good at coaching defensively but honestly, it wasn't for me on a long term basis. Even though things didn't go great, I thoroughly enjoyed working with them.

I went home and on New Year's Eve I got a call from Dave Kitson, asking what my status was. I explained and Dave said that Danny Wilson, the Sheffield United manager, had been asking about me, and would I be interested? It sounded great, and the move was sorted out fairly swiftly on the day. I was taking a hit on my wages but the deal I agreed with United was that if I played 10 games, I'd get an extra year on my contract automatically. As quickly as that, my association with Stoke came to an end.

Danny Wilson called later on and said, "Great to have you on board Danny. We're playing Doncaster tomorrow – can you play?" I replied yeah, but I didn't have any boots! I'd left them at Ipswich as I'd half expected to go back.

Danny went out and got me some boots so I was able to play – it was a difficult introduction, but we recovered from 2-0 down to get a point, Kits equalising in the last minute. They took around 5,000 supporters over there which was an eye opener to how big the club was, despite being in League One. The following week we won at Oxford in the FA Cup so it was a really good start to life there, but it wasn't to last. In my home league debut, we lost 2-0 to a strong Yeovil team that went on to get promoted.

After our form nosedived, Danny lost his job and was replaced in the short term by Chris Morgan. Chris felt it would be best to return to the settled back four that they'd played before I arrived and that was fair enough. I appreciated that he told me straight up. Morgs is only a year older than me and I knew it wasn't an easy job he had, so I said if he needed me to do anything I was more than happy to help out. He took me up on that and asked if I'd help Richard Cresswell coach the under 21s.

Though I wasn't to feature in the play-offs, I was desperate for the lads to do well – I'd played my 10 games, so I'd got another year, and I hoped it would be in the Championship, but it wasn't to be as Yeovil overcame us.

That summer of 2013 was lovely – we spent a lot of time in the garden relaxing.

I'd been through a lot of change after coming back from my cruciate injury. Normally I'd find myself itching to get back but for the first time I found myself not only with little interest in going back, but actually feeling like I didn't want to.

20

The Rock

I believe that things happen for a reason. Not everything. Ill-
nesses, death – I don't mean those tragic events. I mean the
smaller things that make up the journey of your life. Things
that might not necessarily mean something at the time but do
on reflection, no matter how long it takes to connect the dots.

I couldn't have predicted what would happen to me in the late
summer of 2013, but maybe it happened to me for a reason,
just at the time I was struggling with my future as a footballer.

I got a tweet from someone random – I still don't know who
it was – saying that they'd heard I might be available to play
for Gibraltar and asking me if it was true. I replied and said as
far as I knew it was; my mum is Spanish and her mum is from
Gibraltar.

Next thing, Allen Bula, who is my uncle – someone I hadn't seen for around 15 or 16 years when we'd been on a rare holiday to Spain to see my mum's family – sent me a message on Twitter asking if I was free for a chat. I've not been on Twitter long; in fact, I never had any form of social media profile at all up until that point. I had no interest in it.

I've always known I had Gibraltar in my blood. There's always been an allegiance there. But I would be lying if I said that throughout my career it was my aim to play for them. It wasn't a desire of mine at all.

People have asked me in my later years if I was gutted that I never got the call-up for England. Let's be honest now – I was never good enough for that. I couldn't be one of those and say 'if this had happened or that had happened I might have got a call-up'. Don't forget I was eligible for Spain as well. There was more chance of me landing on the moon than being called up for England or Spain. I'm not being disrespectful to myself, I'm just saying it as it is. When I was in good form and Sven-Goran Eriksson was giving caps to everyone, if I was good enough, I'd have got the call then. Look at the centre backs I was up against – Rio Ferdinand, John Terry, Sol Campbell, to name just three at that time. They were unbelievable.

Gibraltar was a different story and after speaking to my parents about the decision to represent them, I began to feel like it was something that was okay and right to do.

As well as Mum's connection, Dad had been in the army out there – in fact, that's how they met. They got married in Gibraltar and their wedding reception (which they could only afford to last for two hours!) was at a place called The Rock Hotel on the island.

At the age of 34, to get an international call-up was weird. Having discussed it with Allen, I made the announcement and the media interest was incredible. The week before, in particular, was crazy with a load of newspaper interviews and MUTV filming me.

The first international game involving Gibraltar to be officially recognised by UEFA was a friendly match against Slovakia in Portugal. Our training camp was at the Algarve Stadium, which was built for Euro 2004.

It might not have been until that point that I finally realised how big a game it was; not because it was me making my international debut, but for everything that it meant for Gibraltar and their people.

Gibraltar first applied for UEFA membership in 1999 but this had been rejected due to Spanish opposition. Spain were afraid it might encourage other areas within their country to stake a claim to be separate. England, Scotland and Wales supported Gibraltar in another vote in 2007 but again it was unsuccessful. Finally, after an appeal, they were accepted as full UEFA members in May, 2013. It had been a long road for them.

The squad had been together for a while and played a number of games that weren't officially recognised so I was joining a fairly established set-up.

I've never been one for a fuss or making a big declaration but on meeting up with them I was asked if I had anything to say. Usually I would have said 'no', but I stood up in front of everyone and said, "Listen. You lot have done the hard work – I appreciate everything you've done in welcoming me, I just want you to understand I've come here to help. I'll give 100 per cent to do whatever I can."

I wanted them to know I hadn't come just to get a cap, no matter what I'm sure some people thought.

I had received some negative comments in the build-up questioning my motivation to be taking part. To be fair, I knew where the cynics were coming from – if I was looking at it from the outside, I'd probably have seen it the same way.

A few years back my old team-mate and manager Roy Keane reportedly made a comment about it being wrong, players winning international caps when they have no real ties to the country they're representing and I'd have to say that's an opinion I agree with. Early on in the 2013/14 season, there was a lot of talk about assimilation and the suggestion that if someone has lived in England for five years then they should be eligible to play for England but I don't agree with that.

If you've got relevant ancestry and family heritage then fine. There are players I don't need to name who have admitted publicly to having no blood ties to the country they've played for. If my grandmother wasn't Gibraltarian I'd have felt like I was a fraud. I don't care if it's Lionel Messi or Cristiano Ronaldo, if they don't have a blood connection to the country they represent then I don't see how it can be justified. There was a lot of talk about Adnan Januzaj representing England soon after he made his Manchester United debut which is the point I'm trying to make.

As we approached the first game, everything at Gibraltar was treated as professionally as it had been at any of the top clubs I'd played at. They were a small nation and accepted that but the structure was in place to cultivate a successful mentality and an established base. Coaches for different areas of the teams, doctors, nutritionists. Everything was spot on and it made for as professional a preparation as anyone could have hoped for.

The build-up on the day of the Slovakia game – Tuesday, November 19th – was a very emotional event to witness. There weren't nerves, it was more of a reverential atmosphere. I couldn't understand that at first. Allen came in and gave his team meeting and government officials made a few speeches. It was really hitting home to me that this was so much more than just playing a game of football. It was the final destination of a long journey.

The match itself was a strange one. In the first ten minutes, a few of our players – perhaps through anxiety – were being gung-ho and trying to get us off to the dream start. Maybe it was my experience but I knew how strong a side we were up against, so I was trying to get the message across to everyone to try and keep our shape, soak up the pressure and be as disciplined as possible.

We managed to do that and held on to what was a fantastic 0-0 result. We might have even pinched it in the end with a late chance, but I don't think that would have been fair, even if it would have been a fairytale. The nearest person to me at the final whistle was the goalkeeper, Jordan Perez. When I went to congratulate him, I saw he was crying. As I approached other team-mates, they were in tears too.

Okay, we'd drawn with Slovakia, who were a really good side, but I felt like I was missing something. I was obviously missing the connection which meant so much. There were hundreds of fans who'd driven from Gibraltar to be there. Gibraltarians are very proud people and as I returned to the dressing room, I saw how it had affected everyone else. More speeches, more tears.

It was incredible to be a part of it. I hadn't been through what they all had; I hadn't banged my head against a brick wall for years like some of them had, but even so, it gave me chills to have been a part of it.

The seven hour coach journey back to Gibraltar flew by. Everyone was still talking about how much it meant. I stayed up until around six in the morning having a couple of drinks and taking it in. Everyone was still wanting to speak to us all and then as I went to the airport to return home there were people still saying thank you and congratulating me. I should have been thanking them.

I hoped at least that my performance persuaded them that I was there for the right reasons. Thankfully, it seemed to; when I received praise for that, it meant a lot to me. In truth, praise or criticism for how well someone thought I'd played would barely have mattered, it was the principle of whether I would be committed. I knew I would be, no question, but I wanted to make sure that others knew that too.

I was able to look myself in the mirror and feel okay with the decision – and the way I've felt since making my debut has justified that. I was immensely proud to do so. It was wholly positive.

If there was a disappointment from the experience it's that even though I'm able to share the story with my friends and family and tell them what happened, they weren't there. There's no way they could have been, realistically, but it was difficult to try and articulate quite how emotional an experience it was. I'd been around historic events in the past at clubs I'd played for – Manchester United became the first ever English 'World Champions' in Tokyo in 1999, and Stoke City reached the FA

Cup final. That's history through achievement which, without wanting to pull it down, is something that people strive towards and is part of the professional aspect of the game.

It almost goes without saying that what I'd just experienced with Gibraltar was something that transcends sport, it was a huge deal for the people culturally and when you are a part of something like that it does affect you. Afterwards I received cards, letters, emails, tweets, all thanking me for being a part of it.

Because Gibraltar is part of the British Territories it was talked about quite a lot back in England. If we'd taken on Slovakia and been beaten five or six nil then we might have just got comments like 'unlucky boys' as if we were just another San Marino, a team of whipping boys.

The result – albeit against a weakened side – made people sit up and take notice. Not only was the draw a reward for those who'd worked so hard to make it happen but it was justification for all their campaigning. Gibraltar were there to compete, not just make up the numbers.

Taking everything into account, I class making my debut for Gibraltar against Slovakia alongside making my full debut for Manchester United against Leicester City as the highlight of my career.

I learnt afterwards that in appearing for Gibraltar I'd broken the record of the oldest Manchester United academy product to make their international debut! I don't know if my name's on the international board at Old Trafford yet.

That in itself is strange, and I suppose it might even tie in with some of the insecurities I felt about being labelled as a Manchester United player.

It's great that I played for United and had that association, and everyone always wants to talk to me and ask me questions about it. But sometimes I get a bit embarrassed – I only played a few games there.

Some years ago, a group of the older players went over to Barbados to play in a Legends tournament and I got a call asking me to join them. I texted Andy Cole and said to him that I didn't deserve to go and play in a 'legends' team with the likes of him and Dwight Yorke. I offered to be their kitman, though! I like to feel that I know my place.

Since then I've worked at MUTV alongside some great names and that feels right. I believe it's not just my connection as a player which is the reason I'm there. It's also because people think my opinions are decent and I've got good things to say.

I've done a few shows with David May and he also asked me to get involved in those tournaments – I could only repeat what I'd said to Andy, that I couldn't justify it alongside players like him who'd played so many times. He insisted that there's a good mix of players with differing first team fortunes, and that has changed my thinking on it. Maybe I'd feel differently if asked in the future but I think I'd still be embarrassed. If it was Stoke, Sunderland, Derby, then okay, I played a decent amount of times for them.

One of the first things I did after announcing my retirement in January, 2014, was call Allen and tell him that I was going to fulfil my promise of playing the next two games for Gibraltar. I was able to train at Nantwich Town and I want to thank the manager, Danny Johnson, who was brilliant to me there. It kept me ticking over so I was in shape when the games came around.

When it came to joining back up with the lads on international duty Allen asked if I might be interested in becoming one of the coaching staff for the forthcoming European Championship qualifying campaign. I thought it was a great opportunity and most of the lads were trying to convince me to play on.

Our group included the likes of Germany, Scotland and Ireland. They would obviously be great occasions to be involved in but I just couldn't justify playing week in, week out for anyone at any level simply so I could be registered to play for Gibraltar. Our friendly against Faroe Islands was a learning curve – we lost 4-1, which showed everyone there was a lot of work to do.

Before the Estonia match in March, Allen pulled me to one side and said he was going to take me off with two or three minutes to go as it was my retirement game. I told him to forget it if it was close – if it was 1-0 to us, or them, going into the late stages, I wasn't going to come off. I'd rather be part of a team that stuck it out and got a result.

Unfortunately we were 2-0 down with 10 minutes left and with a couple of minutes on the clock I was brought off. I got a standing ovation. Everyone was giving me hugs and shaking my hand; even the Estonian players. It was a nice way to go out. Afterwards we went out for a meal and I was presented with a signed shirt and flag – how could I have ended my career any better? An international – seven months prior, that would have been laughable.

It was the stark contrast of being exposed to the thrill of international football as opposed to how I was beginning to feel about playing at club level which served as the major indicator of what was going wrong, and it's no coincidence that everything snowballed in such a short space of time afterwards.

The two games I'd played for Chester before the Gibraltar game were against Hereford and Luton; Luton were top of the league, we drew 1-1 and we should've beaten them. I'd had MUTV following me with the Gibraltar game coming up and I said after that I'd got quite a buzz from that Luton game. Being honest, it wasn't until afterwards I realised that I'd been excited because of the fact I was going to play for Gibraltar.

I'm connected with Gibraltar now. I've learned about the history of the place. I make an effort to stay in contact with everyone in the squad and the FA to try and see what I can do to continue to help.

Making my international debut was an enriching experience both for what it helped me accomplish and what it helped me come to terms with. It helped me to let go. Like I say, maybe some things happen for a reason.

21

Winners & Losers

Looking back on my career, I've been lucky enough to play with and against some of the modern day greats of the game. I remember a match at home to Manchester United on Boxing Day when I was at Sunderland.

We ended up getting beaten 4-0. The result was instantly forgettable, but playing against Cristiano Ronaldo wasn't. At the time, he was in that incredible form which would take him to his first Ballon d'Or.

I'd done a fairly good job against him when I'd played for Southampton but this was something different altogether. He'd made amazing progress not just in his game but physically, too. To observe that progress was phenomenal.

Give great credit to United for assisting with that but the man himself had to be given immense praise for the strides he'd made. He showed that an unwavering dedication can make all the difference.

After leaving Old Trafford I was able to say with some justification that I was a Premier League player on merit and not because of my association with United. I was justified in my decision to leave and not overstay my welcome.

I've had a good, strong career on the basis of my ability. I didn't take the comfortable route and get my arse wiped for me. I never looking like getting in the Manchester United squad, let alone the first team. I'd made a bold call and was rewarded with plenty of first team football at a high level. I tested myself against the best.

I would have to say that Ronaldo was the greatest player I ever shared a pitch with. He's one of the true greats to have played in the Premier League and one of the best ever to play for Manchester United.

It was only in a friendly but I was also fortunate enough to come up against Raul when Stoke played a pre-season match against Real Madrid in July, 2007. I'd seen him of TV, of course, and he'd scored goals left, right and centre. He was widely considered to be the best Real player ever.

As a defender, I was watching thinking 'He's not the quickest. He's not the strongest. How does he do everything that he does?' I found out the hard way. To say I learned a lesson is an understatement. I spent so much time that game running without actually touching the ball and I came off the pitch thinking that his movement was second to none. Unique. I was chasing shadows. This was a pre-season game, too, so it wasn't like he was at his physical peak!

Likewise, I had tough games against greats in Thierry Henry and Dennis Bergkamp. Bergkamp was a lot like Teddy Sheringham, he wasn't blessed with electric pace but it barely mattered as he had five yards in his head. By the time you went to react to what he was going to do, he'd already done it.

Michael Owen was electric, particularly in his earlier years. Then there was Michael Ballack. We once played Bayern Munich at Southampton and Ballack, though a midfielder, was a nightmare to pick up with his clever runs. Alan Shearer was another tough customer. He made backing into the defender and somehow making it look like you fouled him an art form. It was difficult not to fall for it, but I enjoyed my battles with him. Ruud van Nistelrooy, Andy Cole, Dwight Yorke – give these guys only a yard and you'll be punished.

Some of the toughest to play against were not even names as celebrated as the ones I've just mentioned. Paul Dickov was a nightmare. He was all over you like a rash, you never had a second's peace. I was never comfortable playing against him and that's the biggest compliment I can pay him.

I consider myself so fortunate to have tested myself against some big names in the game. I don't think there are many instances in which I was embarrassed by any top players – though admittedly that might have more to do with the fact that I was playing for teams where organisation was key, so I was never really exposed, never isolated.

That's probably credit to the managers I played under, but I always felt I gave a good account of my own ability no matter who it was against. I wasn't a world beater, I was a six or seven out of ten every week but at the same time I was never a problem.

Another great I could mention who compares with any of those names is David Beckham.

In 1998, United had one of those rare summers during that decade when a period of regeneration was required following a year without winning a trophy. Not only was Alex Ferguson concentrating on that, he was also dealing with the fall out of the 1998 World Cup which had seen Beckham controversially sent off against Argentina.

The press had a field day with it. Darren Anderton had started the World Cup ahead of Beckham and the papers were full of journalists asking how Beckham couldn't be in the team. He got his chance against Colombia, did remarkably well, and then Argentina happened and Beckham's face was on mock dartboards while people were burning effigies of him. The storm had followed him back to Manchester and he was having police escorts guiding him to the Cliff for the first few days.

Despite Beckham's status, you just couldn't believe the vitriol that was surrounding him. It was a sad state of affairs. These things can happen. David Beckham wasn't responsible for England losing – let's not forget they got to a penalty shoot-out after he was sent off.

It was an introduction to a world where I realised that, as much as these players were colleagues and sportsmen, there was also a tremendous amount of pressure on them. At United we were taught to deal with that. The manager said in one of his books that a good friend of Fabio Capello told him that even if the players were wearing a cloak and a mask he could still identify which ones played for United, such was their attitude. That rang true for me – I cannot state how important that upbringing was for me, and all the players helped David through that time. It would be no surprise for anyone who knew that squad. It was like a big family. And the man himself dealt with it remarkably well.

People talk about him being concerned with celebrity – what a load of nonsense – he is probably one of the most mentally strong people I have ever seen in my career. He always bounced back from problems stronger, he was a go-to man in your team. He was a leader, different to Roy Keane, but a leader in a different way – as we saw against Greece in 2001. He's the type of player who always wanted the ball, no matter how big the pressure was, and he'd always been like that.

Leaders come in all shapes and forms and that dressing room was full of them. They are people who will grab hold of the game by the scruff of the neck when things aren't going right and it sometimes doesn't have anything to do with the quality of the players. It's no coincidence that you can look at either of United's European Cup-winning teams of 1999 or 2008 and see that they were full of leaders.

Beckham was one in 1998 and his form that season showed it. He's not the only United player to have suffered a backlash from the press because of an England exit at an international tournament. Phil Neville in 2000, Wayne Rooney in 2006. Even Rooney's form in 2010 was cited as a reason. Manchester United have been the premier club in the country for 25 years. When you're at the top you're there to be shot at so that's what happens – it will happen to Manchester City, or Chelsea, whoever is the next team to dominate.

For whatever reason – and it's a mentality I can't come to terms with – people like to see top stars start to struggle. It happens with many things, not just football. Whenever there's a bit of controversy with a footballer, it can be milked for all its worth.

It reminds me of a time when I was at Southampton and I was visiting a local hospital. My eldest son, Jak, was about four at the time and so it really resonates with you as a parent to see ill kids. One of the children we saw was about Jak's age and he was wired up to machines and all sorts. He reached out to his dad and it just struck a chord with me.

I'd never been one for crying a lot but I was uncontrollable for a good hour after that, it just brought the fragility of life home to me. There were two girls, one who suffered from cancer and the other from leukemia. We kept in touch with them, and one of the girls, unbeknown to me, lived around the corner from us and actually went to the same primary school as my son.

I was due to go to a fundraising event for the other one time when we received a call to inform us that she had died – she was only six. They held a charity match for her which I refereed and afterwards I kept in touch with the family just to see if there was anything I could do to help. The other girl began to get better – I'd go and see her quite regularly. With them living locally, one day I bumped into her dad, and asked how she was getting on.

"She's doing really well, it's great what you're doing with coming to see her." "Not at all," I replied. "Anything I can do to help."

"I'm really pissed off – I've been into work and one of the guys says you're just doing it for the publicity."

He knew it wasn't the case. Nobody else knew apart from him and me. If it was to do with the publicity I'd have arranged for the papers to be there. But that was the perception, just because I was a footballer.

Another lad had come over from the Isle of Wight to have a game for Southampton and he collapsed on the pitch. He was in a bad way at the local hospital. I'd ring the parents beforehand to let them know I was planning to go in and to make sure it was a good time.

This time, the boy's dad said he was in a bad way, so I said I would leave it – he insisted I came, as it would be better if I did. Of course, I did as I was asked, and by the end of the visit, he was laughing and playing a guitar.

That, for me, is worth more than anything that you can do in football, but football brings that opportunity. It makes you a role model.

I have been fortunate enough to learn from some great managers and that has continued into my new career too. In the summer of 2014, I travelled with Manchester United to the United States in their early days under Louis van Gaal, a manager as accomplished as any in the modern era.

Observing his methods and man-management ability was a great experience and hopefully will be something that I am able to put to use in my media career.

With all the stress involved in being a manager or a coach (it becomes a 24 hour job) it is not something that tickles my fancy at this stage of my life. One of the reasons I gave up playing was to spend more time with my family, after all.

I don't regret playing on as long as I did. I think I left at the right time and I can certainly say that I tried everything I could to re-ignite the passion I once had for the game but if I'm being truthful then I was starting to enjoy the punditry work a lot more than I was playing.

Much of it was down to circumstance. It was sheer chance that I picked up the injury just after an amazing couple of weeks; my response, to shut everything out, and concentrate on the media work, meant that I saw that as a release, something to put effort in and be passionate about. The seeds were sown as early as 2011.

Months have passed since my retirement and I've been able to enjoy watching my son play football on a Saturday – stood on the sidelines in the pissing rain. I honestly could not be more content.

As soon as I retired, I had a few drinks and the next day I went to the bookies to put a couple of bets on. Drinking and gambling are traditional vices for ex-pros but this was just to let my hair down rather than seeing an opportunity to go off the rails.

It reminded me of when I was at Derby. I was a young lad with no strings and after training, I'd go to the casino. I went so often that they knew my name. One day I won a load, and then the next day I lost it all. I went home and resolved not to go back again, and I was fortunate enough, or strong-willed enough, to stick to it.

It was only a spell of two weeks, but it was enough to put me off – along with another occasion when I was playing cards on the back of the bus on the way to the FA Cup final in 2003. We played Shoot Pontoon and in one fell swoop I lost about about a grand and half. I was stupid but I learned my lesson from those two experiences. Gambling wasn't for me. At Southampton, I did invest in a racehorse with a few of the lads – but it was harmless fun. We went down to the racetrack before it was being renovated. I got a bit worse for wear and decided that I was going to run the track. I was the last ever living thing to run the final furlong on that track! Rory wanted to pinch the finishing line post but the steward took it off him.

I don't want to make light of what is obviously a very traumatic problem for many other people; in dressing rooms, you would find that those who did have a problem would keep it hidden. You'd only find out about it when it was leaked into the public domain.

It's a dangerous thing, as footballers have a lot of time on their hands and some veer off the straight and narrow. It is a risk, of course. When players end their careers, they have a lot of time on their hands. That's why I consider myself so lucky that first and foremost I have the time to spend with my family who I love to pieces and secondly that I have been so fortunate to find a second career, so soon, which has replaced the excitement of playing football.

If I'm working on a big game then I get the buzz, a similar buzz to how it was when I played, and the night before I can barely sleep with all the thoughts running around my head.

Football has been my life. I wouldn't call it a regret but it is a lament that I never actually won anything… as I've said, I don't count the medals that I did receive as I never took part.

Pubs and bars are full of sob stories – could've, would've, should've. People who wish they were players. Even players who wish they could've done more.

In a strange way, though, I'm proud of everything I've done. People talk about winners and losers, about who is successful and who is a failure but the only truth is what's inside your own head. I'm content with what I achieved and who I am. Maybe that's worth more than a medal or two.

I don't want to be known primarily as an 'ex-footballer'. It's just not my way… I'd much rather be remembered, or should I say known, for what I'm doing in the present tense. I'll be grateful if fans come up to me and say they remember me as a player but I'll get far more satisfaction if they approach me to say they've agreed with an opinion I've given in the media.

It's important to be able to move on. I was able to adapt and survive after leaving United. I did the same at other points in my career. That's what you have to do. Always pick yourself up after you've had a fall.

I hope I gave something to the fans of the clubs I played for. If we proved a few people wrong, upset the odds and raised their hopes – even for a day – then it was all worth it. But I've created a new life for myself now.

I'm writing these as the final lines of my autobiography but in all honesty I feel like I'm at the start of a career rather than at the end of one; like an apprentice, unsure of what to expect but knowing I'll have to give it my all.

It's been a fantastic journey so far – and there's plenty of road left to travel.

About Danny Higginbotham

Danny Higginbotham has built a successful career in the media following his retirement from professional football in 2014.

He has worked for Sky, BBC 5 live and has written for the Manchester Evening News.

Currently, he works for BT Sport, Talksport, the BBC, MUTV, Premier League Productions and BreatheSport. He writes for The Independent and The Sentinel.

www.tripleamedia.com

RISE
OF THE
UNDERDOG

Sport Media